Business incubation: boon or boondoggle?

Alice M. Flannigan

Abstract

Business incubators, a popular entrepreneurship policy intended to help new businesses avoid the risks of failure and generate economic growth, now serve more than 1,600 communities across the United States. Business incubators help new ventures by providing subsidized office space, shared administrative services, access to capital and financing, networking opportunities, and assistance with legal, technology transfer, and export procedures. Despite the widespread existence of business incubators, little systematic knowledge exists detailing whether incubators help new ventures improve their business performance. This dissertation investigates two questions: 1) Do incubated firms outperform their unincubated peers? And 2) Does the economic performance of incubated firms vary according to design characteristics of incubators and attributes of the entrepreneur? These studies rely on a sample of approximately 950 business incubators, 19,000 incubated businesses, and a matched control group of unincubated businesses. Measures of new venture performance include survival, employment growth, and sales growth. Overall, this dissertation concludes that business incubation lowers the expected lifespan of incubated businesses while increasing their employment and sales growth rates. Additionally, this dissertation finds that certain types of business incubators create better-performing new ventures and that women owned firms benefit more from incubation than men owned firms.

Contents

Chapter 1

Introduction

Business incubators have long been a powerful tool for helping new businesses launch and existing firms grow. In 2005 alone, incubators assisted 27,000 start-up companies that provided full-time employment for over 100,000 Americans and generated $17 billion in revenue.

— Congresswoman Nydia M. Velázquez, 12th District, New York
March 17, 2010 hearing of the House Committee on Small Business

Since the 1980s, communities across the U.S. have seized on promoting entrepreneurship as a key to economic growth. This interest in entrepreneurship is reflected in the explosive growth of business incubators—institutions that provide subsidized space and management support to new ventures, which grew from 12 in 1980 to over 1,400 today (Knopp, 2007). Incubators thrive because of the underlying belief that that they select and nurture good business ideas that generate economic growth. But do they?

At the moment, few peer-reviewed studies exist that empirically evaluate the impact of business incubation on new venture performance. Yet, the National Business Incubation Association (NBIA) claims that business incubation is unequivocally a better investment of scarce economic development dollars than other types of programs. NBIA cites in-house research showing that for every $1 of public funding received by an incubator, its tenants and former tenants generate approximately $30

"

in local tax revenue (Molnar, 1997). These statistics come from NBIA's own analysis of internal surveys of its members, which lack a scientific data collection process and rigorous estimation methods (Knopp, 2007; Linder, 2002). Furthermore, NBIA is now citing a recent study by the Economic Development Administration (EDA) that shows that business incubators generate 20 times more permanent employment than construction capital projects like roads and bridges (Arena, Adams, Noyes, Rhody, & Noonan, 2008). Yet, the EDA study fails to present regression results despite claiming that regression methods were used. If true, NBIA's and EDA's estimates of the contribution of incubated businesses to local economies would clearly encourage the expanded use of incubators. However, scholarly attention is needed to confirm these conclusions and provide guidance to the incubation industry in order to improve on the past success of these programs.

As communities across the country struggle through an unprecedented recession and the atrophy of industrial manufacturing economies (Audretsch, 2007), policymakers and economic development experts are eager to implement policies that can build a prosperous future for their citizens. For decades, policymakers and the incubation industry have sought to know whether economic development programs and policies targeting entrepreneurs increase economic growth in local economies. Yet as others have noted, there is a lack of peer-reviewed research on the topic (Hackett & Dilts, 2004; Sherman & Chappell, 1998) and much concern about the validity of the NBIA's (Bearse, 1998) and the EDA's own research.

1.1 Scholarly Research, Policymakers, and the Incubation Industry

The lack of scholarly attention to this question can be attributed in part to the difficulty of gathering sufficient longitudinal data to determine whether programs like business incubation work. This has left the incubation industry and important government agencies on their own to study and determine the effects of incubation on firm performance and economic growth. While state and local governments continually encourage their own agencies to study the question of incubation's impact, few empirical milestones have been achieved.

For example, in 2001 the State of Maryland conducted a small study on 6 business incubators that found that incubated business in Maryland grew by 33% in terms of employment in a two year period (RESI, 2001). However, this study lacked a comparison control group and failed to interpret the results in relationship to the performance of average new businesses in the state. Many efforts to study the effects of business incubation on tenant performance ignore selection bias, omit comparable control groups, and lack proper estimation techniques.

When the Washington State legislature requested one of its research units evaluate the impact of its 3-year-old policy supporting business incubators, the authors concluded that they could not even identify the exact number of business incubators in the state, much less conduct a robust evaluation that compared incubated and unincubated businesses (Woolley, Konopaski, & Fanning, 2007). This conclusion is startling given that the state created a statutory definition of incubators and has invested approximately $5.6 million over eight years in incubation programs.

What sound research does exist has been contradictory or inconclusive. Allen and Bazan (1990) used a convenience sample of unincubated manufacturing and service sector firms in Pennsylvania to compare with the results of a statewide survey of tenants of business incubators. Allen and Bazan found that incubated businesses did not perform better than the comparison group, especially in terms of employment, sales, and asset growth (Allen & Bazan, 1990). However, when tenants were asked if they thought incubation services were helpful, they overwhelmingly responded positively (Allen & Bazan, 1990).

For a public policy that receives tremendous attention from national, state, and local governments and over \$497 million annually to finance operations and expansion of programs (Linder, 2002), little is known about incubation's effectiveness or its benefits to society. This dissertation addresses the lack of empirical research on the effectiveness of business incubation programs by answering two questions:

1. Do incubated businesses outperform their unincubated peers?

2. Does the economic performance of incubated businesses vary according to design characteristics of incubators and attributes of the entrepreneur?

To answer the first question, I gathered the most comprehensive sample of business incubators and incubated businesses ever assembled and compared the performance of incubated firms to a matched control group of unincubated businesses. I evaluated differences in performance by studying survival, employment growth, and sales growth among incubated and unincubated businesses, using panel method estimation techniques that controlled for location, time, industry, and firm fixed effects.

The second question of this dissertation probes whether idiosyncratic characteristics of incubators and entrepreneurs influence the performance of incubated businesses. This question places emphasis on the effectiveness of incubation practices rather than on the effectiveness of incubation as public policy. To answer this second question, I relied on the same sample of incubators and incubated businesses. Estimation techniques in this study relied on panel data methods that enabled estimation of time invariant characteristics of incubators and entrepreneurs, which were potentially correlated with the unobserved characteristics of incubated businesses.

1.2 Implications and Theoretical Relevance

The purpose of this dissertation is to estimate the effects of incubation on the performance of new businesses, both informing entrepreneurship and economic development policymaking and the practice of business incubation. In addition, the two studies within this dissertation use reliable data and robust estimation techniques that have never before been attempted in the study of business incubation.

Theoretically, these studies advance research on organizational evolutionary theory and knowledge spillover theory. Evolutionary theory posits that the processes of firm selection and retention occur at two levels: internally within organizations and externally in the environment. While internal selection protects an organization from the pressures of the external environment that lead firms to failure, internal selection can also stymie a firm's ability to adapt to a competitive external environment (Aldrich, 1999). Hence, while incubation might insulate a firm from competitive forces of the external environment and increase its likelihood of short-term survival, incubation could also weaken the firm's ability to compete and survive once it leaves the incubator. If incubation were to hurt a firm's likelihood to survive and compete in the market, it would imply that a government program intended to address a possible market failure actually decreased economic efficiency, thus calling into question the role of government intervention in the market when the public good that is desired—employment and economic growth—is actually being diminished (Arrow, 1962).

From the perspective of theories on knowledge spillovers, this study speaks to the call to adapt economic development policies so that they foster economic growth that exploits locally produced knowledge whose economic value is most easily captured by those with close proximity to sources of research (Audretsch, Keilbach, & Lehmann, 2006). This policy prescription contrasts with prior economic development strategies that emphasized fiscal incentives and that subsidized incumbent firms (Bartik, Boehm, & Schlottmann, 2003), as opposed to new business development. Research on entrepreneurship and knowledge spillovers has uncovered several market failures that potentially impede entrepreneurial activity: the lack of knowledge production, low social network densities, a preponderance to ignore the learning from failed ventures, and cultural preferences that discourage individuals from pursuing careers as entrepreneurs (Audretsch, Keilbach *et al.*, 2006). In Chapter 5, I investigate directly the ability of incubators to reduce barriers to entrepreneurship through their collaborations with institutions of higher education and with networks in the business community.

1.3 Outline

In the chapters that follow, I first review key literature on entrepreneurship, economic development, and business incubation to place this dissertation at the nexus of entrepreneurship research and economic development policy. In addition, I summarize key studies on business incubators in the scholarly literature. I emphasize methods and findings that have attempted to answer the question of whether business incubation works and how its practices relate to tenant performance. This chapter concludes that just as government-hired policy analysts have struggled to adequately study the impact of business incubation on firm performance, so have scholars.

In Chapter 3, I outline the methods I used to collect data on incubators, incubated businesses, and a matched control group of unincubated firms. The chapter discusses how data on all three groups of organizations was cleaned up, verified, and merged into one master time-series dataset. This section also illustrates key descriptive statistics on all three groups of organizations.

Chapter 4 presents the theory, methods, and findings of the study that investigates whether incubated businesses outperform their unincubated peers during incubation and post-incubation.

Chapter 5 looks at the question of whether the economic performance of incubated businesses varies according to design characteristics of incubators and unique characteristics of the entrepreneur.

Finally, Chapter 6 summarizes the results of the dissertation, discusses their implications, and presents ideas for future research on this topic. Overall, this dissertation found that the effect of incubation on the performance of incubated businesses is marginal when compared with the performance of unincubated businesses. In other words, incubation is not associated with a major increase in the survival, employment growth, and sales growth of new ventures. However, the analysis on how traits of an incubator and the entrepreneur were associated with the performance of incubated businesses did find noteworthy evidence that some types of incubators perform better than others.

Chapter 2

A Review of Entrepreneurship, Economic Growth, and Incubation Literature

> You could think of an incubator as a university of a kind, where the incubator manager is very careful in selecting the right companies to come in and gain access to comprehensive services that help improve the sustainability of these firms. Incubator clients usually stay for about a two- or three-year period of time, depending on the industry they operate in. They expect to graduate, having internalized the assistance over time, too. They are going to graduate, and there are strong indications that they stay also in their industry; they stay in their communities for time afterwards.
>
> — DAVID MONKMAN, President & CEO, National Business Incubation Assn.
> March 17, 2010 hearing of the House Committee on Small Business

A business incubator is an organization that supports the creation and growth of new businesses by providing subsidized office space, shared administrative services, access to capital and financing, networking opportunities, and assistance with legal, technology transfer, and export procedures (Allen & Weinberg, 1988; Erlewine & Gerl, 2004; Hackett & Dilts, 2004). Although local governments use a variety of policy tools such as taxation, enterprise zones, and small business development centers to retain, attract, and create businesses (Bartik, 2003; Bartik, 2005), this study focuses on business incubation because of its prevalence across urban and rural communities. In addition, business incubators operate as nonprofit and for-profit entities, inside universities and as standalone organizations, and often focus on niche industries. The diversity of practices and configurations of business incubators motivates research on policy, program management, and strategy to improve understanding of how incubation helps new businesses and how incubation services could increase their performance.

This dissertation views incubation as a type of entrepreneurship policy that alters competitive forces in the private market in order to promote public welfare. In other words, I am examining the effect of public intervention, through business incubation, on the growth and survival of private businesses. The study of business incubation allows for a better assessment of the achievements or failures of policymakers to understand a complex technological, social, and economic phenomenon such as entrepreneurship.

In this chapter, I outline entrepreneurship as a process (Gartner, Carland, Hoy, & Carland, 1988), explain relevant entrepreneurship policies at the local level, and discuss the state of research on business incubation. The goal is to explain entrepreneurship as a phenomenon, discuss the role of policy in mediating the behavior of this phenomenon, and offer some thoughts about the construct of business incubation in order to inform evaluation of data in later chapters.

2.1 Entrepreneurship: Actions, Individuals, and Firms

Entrepreneurship is a phenomenon that involves the creation of opportunities and "individuals who discover, evaluate, and exploit them" (Shane & Venkataraman,

2000). As an action, entrepreneurship results when individuals act to produce a new good, improve the quality of a current good, adopt a more efficient method of production, open new markets for an already available good or service, discover and control a new supply of raw materials, and/or alter the competitive dimensions of an industry (Baumol, 1993; Schumpeter, 1934). Entrepreneurs pursue these actions in their quest for wealth, power, and position (Baumol, 1993) and their actions lead to the creation of new organizations (Gartner, Carland *et al.*, 1988).

Because entrepreneurship is a phenomenon carried out by both individuals and firms, its explanation and theories are an amalgamation of various disciplines (Audretsch, Grilo, & Thurik, 2007). Hence, many of the theoretical explanations of how entrepreneurship varies across regions and time (Audretsch, Grilo *et al.*, 2007; Verheul, Wennekers, Audretsch, & Thurik, 2002) tend to offer exhaustive and technical presentations that cover a range of issues such as level of analysis, demand and supply models of entrepreneurship, and the stages of entrepreneurship. I take the view that entrepreneurship manifests itself in specific behaviors and conditions known to be necessary for individuals to pursue entrepreneurial ventures. Thus, I adopt Shane's (2003) general theory of entrepreneurship as a starting point for defining entrepreneurship. I choose this theory because it describes the circumstances and actions necessary for individuals and firms to pursue entrepreneurship. It is a theory that succinctly summarizes the policy, psychological, management, and economic theories that explain entrepreneurial activity. Yet, these theories on their own fail to encompass the full spectrum of activities and decisions that result in entrepreneurship (Shane, 2003).

Additionally, I assume that entrepreneurs are not created (Baumol, 1993). They always exist in society and their traits and characteristics are difficult to differentiate from those of other small business owners and other relevant groups in the population (Gartner, Carland *et al.*, 1988). However, entrepreneurs can be categorized and government policy can encourage pursuit of productive types of economic activities as opposed to unproductive ones (Baumol, 1990). Productive activities are those that increase economic outputs by generating new products or services, lowering costs of existing production processes, improving the quality of existing products or services, increase the supply of raw materials, and/or alter the structure of an industry (Schumpeter, 1934). Unlike unproductive forms of entrepreneurship that generate profits from rent-seeking behavior, productive activities increase supplies of goods and services by generation more value in the economy (Baumol, 1993). Rent-seeking implies receiving payments for activities that do not increase supplies of transacted goods or services; thus, rents raise the cost to society for a good without eventually leading to increased supplies and new entrants into a competitive market. Unproductive entrepreneurship describes cases where prevailing norms, regulations, and economic transactions allow an individual to profit without that individual needing to incur equivalent costs (Baumol, 1993).

Hence, in this study, I view entrepreneurship as a process (Shane, 2003) that results in new firm creation (Gartner, 1985) where individuals either engage in productive or unproductive types of activities (Baumol, 1993). Because society benefits from increased economic growth, entrepreneurship is a phenomenon that deserves public policy attention and has garnered significant policymaking interest in recent times (Ács & Stough, 2008). Hence, this dissertation looks at how business incubation, one common type of entrepreneurship public policy, affects the creation, growth, and sustainability of new firms. However, an unanswered question in this dissertation is whether business incubation leads to productive entrepreneurship as opposed to unproductive entrepreneurship.

2.2 The Six Processes of Entrepreneurship and Related Public Policies

In the general theory of entrepreneurship, Shane (2003) explains that entrepreneurship occurs at the nexus of enterprising individuals and valuable opportunities. Entrepreneurship occurs when individuals discover and evaluate created opportunities that can potentially generate greater economic value than currently existing ventures (Shane, 2003). Nevertheless, entrepreneurship only develops when individuals subsequently decide to exploit the assessed opportunity by financing, organizing, and developing a strategy that becomes a sustainable and profitable new venture (Shane, 2003). In this section, I briefly explain each process and related policies.

Opportunity Creation

Opportunities materialize when "new goods, services, raw materials, and organizing methods can be introduced and sold" at a profit (Shane & Venkataraman, 2000). Scientific research and inventions serendipitously lead to the creation of new raw materials, technologies, and processes with potential economic value (Mokyr, 1990; Shane, 2003). In addition, entrepreneurial opportunities emerge when society experiences political, regulatory, and demographic changes (Baumol, 1993; Shane & Venkataraman, 2000). Entrepreneurial opportunities require the creation of new means–ends relationships and hence differ from mainstream profit-making opportunities, which essentially focus on generating efficiencies and optimizing current processes (Eckhardt & Shane, 2003; Shane & Venkataraman, 2000).

Two public policies believed to generate entrepreneurial opportunities include investments in R&D and deregulation. Opportunity creation through scientific research is often risky and may generate greater returns to society than to private firms (Mansfield, Rapoport, Romeo, Wagner, & Beardsley, 1977). Thus, public investments in R&D are often advocated to encourage opportunity creation (Arrow, 1962). Alternatively, changes to regulations, especially deregulation, have been hypothesized to increase opportunities by lowering barriers to entry (Capelleras, Mole, Greene, & Storey, 2008; Soto, 2000). It is important to note that opportunity creation initiates a chain of events that leads an individual or firm to engage in entrepreneurship.

Opportunity Discovery

A key tenet of the general theory of entrepreneurship is that entrepreneurs make non-optimizing decisions. In other words, when entrepreneurs market a new good or service, by default the price system fails to provide the necessary information to optimize prices and supplies of the good or service being sold. When entrepreneurs lack market information about the value of a future good, service, or process, they must act on a belief that profit is attainable through the buying, selling, or transformation of resources in a new manner (Shane, 2003). This belief—a discovered opportunity—is the product of subjective cognitive processes (Shane, 2003) which arises because people hold different information and values. Thus, when individuals make conjectures about the value of resources used in a new way and act on those conjectures, and markets then prove willing to pay for a different use of existing and new resources (Shane & Venkataraman, 2000), they have discovered a new opportunity. While the evidence of a successful opportunity is profitability, the evidence of a discovery need not entail a risky venture. Opportunity discovery is simply originating a new conjecture about an unproven and untested mode of production that results in a new product or service.

Factors influencing an individual's discovery of opportunities center on two key variables: idiosyncratic abilities and access to knowledge and information. Psychological studies of entrepreneurs have shown that differences in absorptive capacity among individuals affect their ability to recognize opportunities (Shane, 2000). Those who can consume and process more types and volume of information are more likely to discover entrepreneurial opportunities (Shane, 2003). On the other hand, access to knowledge and information is important because sometimes the most economically valuable opportunities are novel, timely, and not equally distributed (Shane, 2003). Factors that improve one's access to information include previous life experience, social networks, and information clearinghouses.

Thus, public policies that elevate the education and technical experience of individuals play a role in enabling opportunity discovery. In addition, policies that facilitate access to information and new knowledge make it possible for individuals to come across novel new ideas and techniques that could be applied to new modes of production.

Opportunity Evaluation

Just because someone creates and/or discovers an opportunity does not imply that she will act to exploit it (McMullen & Shepherd, 2006). Those creating and discovering opportunities often abandon them so that others can explore and exploit them. Shane (2003) frames the decision to exploit an opportunity as corresponding with the evaluation of three major factors: 1) individual differences, especially non-psychological and psychological factors, 2) industry characteristics, and 3) the institutional environment. Examples of these three factors include individual differences in tolerance for risk and ambiguity, the competitiveness and development of the industry where the opportunity has an advantage, and legal barriers that impede exploitation.

The decision to exploit an opportunity requires evaluating individual, industry, and market factors to determine whether the expected value associated with starting a new venture is worth assuming the financial and personal risks of failure (Abdesselam, Bonnet, & Le Pape, 2004; Shane & Venkataraman, 2000). Essentially, evaluation of an opportunity entails an opportunity cost calculation to determine whether the expected value of becoming an entrepreneur is worth the risk of changing one's current role in the market (Amit, Muller, & Cockburn, 1995).

Factors that individuals weigh when deciding whether to assume the risks of entrepreneurship include the potential loss of income, health care benefits, and lifestyle preferences. Thus, when governments enact policies that make social welfare more equitable between the self-employed and wage earners, important risks assumed by entrepreneurs are lowered (Verheul, Wennekers *et al.*, 2002).

Start-up Financing

In order to start a new venture, entrepreneurs require working capital (Ács & Stough, 2008). Often, entrepreneurs discover, evaluate, and decide to pursue an entrepreneurial opportunity but fail to bring that opportunity to market because they lack start-up financing. Uncertainty and information asymmetry between entrepreneurs and investors (Shane, 2003) often present challenges in securing financing. Thus, the more options society makes available for institutions and individuals to invest in and mitigate economic uncertainties, the more likely it is that discovered opportunities are pursued.

However, as Baumol (1993) argues, society through customs and policy can create incentives for entrepreneurs to pursue opportunities that exploit rent-seeking as opposed to productive activities that increase output and supplies. As has been seen in the recent economic downturn, this area of policy is one that leads to unintended consequences if society is not vigilant towards monitoring rent-seeking behaviors. Nevertheless, public policies designed to ease financing barriers and increase investments in opportunity exploitation include venture capital, direct public financing, bank lending, foreign direct investments, and angel investing (Ács & Stough, 2008; Shane, 2003).

Entrepreneurship Strategy

Once an entrepreneurial venture emerges, owners and managers need to devise a strategy to achieve and maintain a competitive advantage (Shane 2003). In the entrepreneurship process, this implies keeping information about innovations secret, erecting market barriers, and developing contingencies and heuristics to manage uncertainty (Shane 2003). Strategies that firms enact to develop a competitive advantage can include starting small, acquiring other ventures to reduce demand, patenting, and continually innovating. Types of policies that support the development of a successful entrepreneurship strategy include improving patent laws, erecting trade barriers, and helping firms and industries achieve economies of scale (Shane, 2003).

Organizing

Once entrepreneurs begin production, organizing activities are crucial to generating and sustaining profits. Organizing takes place over time and includes activities such as hiring, setting up legal entities, and establishing production processes. The organizing experience is dynamic and the entrepreneur draws from previous education and work experience or imitates other successful firms (DiMaggio & Powell, 1983; Hannan & Freeman, 1977). The key objective of the organizing stage is "to obtain and preserve private value from the exploitation of opportunities" (Shane, 2003, p. 194) by creating complementary routines and structures to match strategies. Public policies related to this stage include those that offer management assistance and training to entrepreneurs through institutions like business incubators and small business development centers.

2.3 Entrepreneurship Policy at the Local Level

Despite the breadth of the entrepreneurship process, local governments are increasingly regarded as shouldering the majority of the responsibility for economic development (Bartik, 2003). While economic development policies can focus on attracting large business operations and retaining current businesses, they have increasingly focused on new business development as well (Bartik, 2003). This has occurred as the U.S. has shifted from an industrialized economy to an entrepreneurial economy based on knowledge production and the exploitation of knowledge resources (Ács & Stough,

2008; Audretsch, 2007).

The shift by local governments towards entrepreneurship is wise, given research indicating that the success of entrepreneurship policy depends largely on its design aligning with the local context (Audretsch, Keilbach, & Lehmann, 2006; Barrios & Barrios, 2004). Sadly, assessments of entrepreneurship policy also reveal that policymakers appear to ignore this link (Cox, Daily, & Pajari, 1991; Hart, 2003). Often, entrepreneurship policy at the local level is described as following a piecemeal approach where a mix of programs are created without paying attention to how they complement each other or the weaknesses of a community (Hart, 2003).

Interest in entrepreneurship by local governments grew when Birch (1987) argued that new businesses, as opposed to large-scale manufacturing, made higher contributions in the form of employment to economic growth. This view challenged a dominant consensus that saw large firms as the sources of economic growth and technological development. While Birch's work has been challenged on methodological grounds, several subsequent studies have begun to piece together evidence supporting his conclusion (Henrekson & Johansson, 2009; Robbins, Pantuosco, Parker, & Fuller, 2000; van Praag & Versloot, 2007).

Small business scholars are finding that regions with higher percentages of very small businesses—firms with less than 20 employees—are characterized by a more productive workforce, more growth in GDP, and lower wage inflation and rates of unemployment (Robbins, Pantuosco *et al.*, 2000). Studies on new and small firms find that small businesses do not hire the vast majority of those employed but that they do produce a majority of new jobs, and more jobs than would be expected solely from large firms (Haltiwanger, 2006). Prior to Birch's research on employment, scholars and policymakers believed that small businesses dabbled marginally in R&D, lacked efficient operations, and offered below-market wages (Audretsch, Keilbach *et al.*, 2006). Today, scholars are finding that new firms play an important role in economic development, especially in entrepreneurial activities (Ács & Armington, 2006; Audretsch, Keilbach *et al.*, 2006).

Because local governments are increasingly noting the positive impact of new business creation on economic development, I will briefly survey the types of policies they have created to stimulate new business development and empirical research on their impact. These local-level entrepreneurship policies include entrepreneurship training, small business advice, capital market programs, and business incubators.

Entrepreneurship training programs

Entrepreneurship training programs seek to provide individuals with entrepreneurial, professional, and business management skills so that they can become self-employed and start new businesses (Doub & Edgcomb, 2005). Entrepreneurship training and education differs from traditional business management training in that it emphasizes the challenges new businesses face at entry (Kuratko, 2005). Interest in entrepreneurship training has grown rapidly in university settings (Kuratko, 2005) as well as in social welfare programs (Klein, Alisultanov, & Blair, 2003). Local governments have become involved as policymakers have learned the effect of entrepreneurship on economic growth and as evidence has grown suggesting that certain types of training, such as business planning, can have a positive impact on new venture success (Shane, 2003). In addition, entrepreneurship programs often target disadvantaged populations, such as the unemployed, minorities, women, veterans, and the disabled (Bartik, 2003; Fairlie & Robb, 2008). Support for such programs stems from studies that suggest that education and training in entrepreneurship can increase the quality and quantity of entrepreneurs in an economy (Matlay, 2006).

The strongest evidence that entrepreneurship training programs work comes from a pilot study of Project GATE (Growing America Through Entrepreneurship) sponsored by the U.S. Department of Labor and the Small Business Administration

(Michaelides & Benus, 2010). Project GATE was administered in three states—Pennsylvania, Minnesota, and Maine—and it randomly assigned applicants to a treatment or control group. The treatment group received an array of self-employment services—classes, workshops, seminars, and counseling—to help them understand how to start, finance, and manage a business. The control group received no services (Michaelides & Benus, 2010).

Results from the study show that the treatment group was more likely to start a business, maintain the business in operation, and/or become self-employed if the individual was unemployed at the time. The program had no effect on the entrepreneurial activities of those already self-employed prior to receiving Project GATE services. The limited conclusion that can be drawn from Project GATE is that entrepreneurship training makes most sense for unemployed individuals seeking to start a business or become self-employed (Michaelides & Benus, 2010). However, because studies like this are rare, it is hard to generalize the value and effectiveness of entrepreneurship training across all local jurisdictions.

Small business advice

The notion that outside assistance is a valuable source of knowledge to entrepreneurs (Chrisman & McMullan, 2004) is a key reason for programs that offer small businesses advice. In the U.S., Small Business Development Centers funded partly by the Small Business Administration are a key purveyor of business planning and counseling services (Bartik, 2003). Over 1,000 of these centers exist across the nation and they provide counseling to small businesses on business development, start-up processes, financing options, and operations (Bartik, 2003). Annually, these centers serve approximately 250,000 small business owners, nascent entrepreneurs, and self-employed individuals (Bartik, 2003). Research indicates that the value of small business advice is not necessarily the knowledge and information conveyed by the counselor but the learning made by the entrepreneur in discussing a business challenge with a business expert (Chrisman & McMullan, 2004).

Other studies reveal that small business advice programs benefit entrepreneurs (Bartik, 2003). However, some of these studies have been challenged due to their design. Unlike a random experimental design, most studies on small business advice programs look at those individuals who self-select to receive such services (Chrisman & McMullan, 2004) and measurement of program effectiveness often relies on survey measurements which may not fully capture true business and service performance (Bartik, 2003). Additionally, Chrisman, the main scholar in this area, has conducted research primarily on behalf of the Small Business Administration. Despite these drawbacks in evaluating small business advice programs, the best research on this topic signals that these programs work. Chrisman & McMullan (2004) find that new businesses that seek outside counseling in their start-up phase tend to survive for longer than the general population of new businesses. These scholars also find that the longer a new venture receives counseling the better its odds of survival. Additionally, they find diminishing returns to the time a new business receives small business advice (Chrisman & McMullan, 2004). Thus, small business advice tends to help a new business with increased results over time but its effect is not sustainable in perpetuity.

Capital market programs

Support for capital financing programs often receives much attention from local policymakers because many entrepreneurs struggle to find adequate financing to exploit discovered entrepreneurial opportunities (Doub & Edgcomb, 2005; Fritsch, 2007; Klein, Alisultanov *et al.*, 2003; Shane, 2003). Increasing sources of capital for new business development is critical given estimates that 90% of new businesses fail within three years if they don't attract venture capital (Gompers & Lerner, 2001, p. 21).

Furthermore, capital market programs at the local level exist because the Small Business Administration plays a central role in sponsoring, subsidizing, and guaranteeing a variety of programs that finance small businesses (Bartik, 2003; Fairlie & Robb, 2008).

In the private sector, debt and equity investing have emerged as the dominant financing instruments available to small and young firms. Institutions offering debt-financing profit from interest accrued on loan repayments while equity investors such as venture capitalists profit from the increased value of their ownership stake in small and young firms (Audretsch, Keilbach *et al.*, 2006). New businesses reap additional benefits from equity investments since venture capitalists often play a critical role in their management.

Evidence of the benefits of venture capital markets comes from Gompers and Lerner (2004), who find that venture capital investments raise the performance of new firms. Their study compares the performance of all venture-backed and non–venture-backed IPOs from 1972 to 1992 and shows that those IPOs backed by venture capital earned 22.1% more than IPOs with no venture capital financing.

However, the findings on venture capital investing have not all been positive. Empirical evidence exists showing that venture capital sometimes decreases some types of business performance, such as sales growth (Bottazzi & Da Rin, 2005), and that it has a much smaller effect on firm performance than often assumed (Zucker, Darby, & Armstrong, 2002). Additionally, some have argued that the benefits of venture capital derive from increased innovation and not increased business performance (Zucker, Darby *et al.*, 2002). Firms receiving venture capital do so because of their novel and attractive research and not because of evidence of their business performance (Zucker, Darby *et al.*, 2002). Regardless, what does appear to be a clear outcome of capital investments on new business performance is that the increased resources acquired by the firm allow it to accumulate a larger stock of strategic assets than its peers over the long run, thus making the firm more likely to survive (Lee, Lee, & Pennings, 2001).

While capital markets in the private sector appear to benefit entrepreneurs, it is less clear whether public capital programs have similar effects. Two reasons posited by Bartik (2004) for why local government financing may not work are the levels of risk that these programs are willing to accept and political pressures that may compromise investment decisions. If public programs are unwilling to assume high levels of risk they may unintentionally end up increasing business activity by simply reducing business activity in another related market—a zero sum game. Additionally, by not investing in higher risk markets, public programs may inhibit the growth of business opportunities that are too risky to garner private financing (Bartik, 2003). Thus, instead of increasing the overall pool of economic activity by investing at the margins, public programs may simply create unproductive competition in existing markets.

Business incubators

Among the various forms of assistance and policies that local governments enact to encourage new business formations, business incubators tend to be the most selective and involved. This is because services of incubators are limited to available physical space and receiving their services entails formal applications, ongoing training and counseling, and monitored exit processes (Linder, 2002).

Incubation is also the most locally focused of these policies. Incubation seeks to increase the number and variety of local businesses by helping entrepreneurs exploit untested opportunities through training, access to financial resources, and mentoring. Often, many of the services that incubators provide overlap with those of small business development centers and entrepreneurship training programs. In many cases, incubators and these other new-business development programs collaborate to help each other's clients. However, the key distinguishing feature and advantage to business incubation is access to cheap and subsidized space (Bartik, 2003; Erlewine & Gerl, 2004; Hackett & Dilts, 2004).

According to the latest national incubation survey, the typical incubator provides direct assistance to an average of 22 businesses (Linder, 2002). In 2002, the total number of existing business incubators was estimated to be 950, with the majority incorporated as nonprofit organizations (Bartik, 2003). Although many incubators charge for some of their services and leased space, most require ongoing operating subsidies (Bartik, 2003). While evaluations of tenants of business incubators often conclude that incubation is important to tenants' success, thus far we do not know whether these successes generate new growth or simply funnel economic activity from unincubated businesses to tenants of incubators who enjoy a unique advantage.

2.4   Business Incubation Research

Previous incubation research has generated few findings due to ambiguous definitions of incubators and the incubation process, inconsistent taxonomies of incubators, and unreliable measures of incubation outcomes (Hackett & Dilts, 2004). To overcome ambiguity regarding the characteristics, performance objectives, and operating policies of incubators, which has hindered generalization of empirical research and theory development within the incubation field (Hackett & Dilts, 2004), this study measures and controls for several key attributes of business incubators. In addition, this study uses a strict definition of business incubation that requires the provision of physical operating space to new businesses, thus avoiding some of the recently created virtual models of business incubation (Carayannis & Zedtwitz, 2005; Zedtwitz & Grimaldi, 2006).

One explanation for the lack of valid and generalizable results across the incubator industry is the complexity of the startup process and the contextual differences between business incubators (Sherman & Chappell, 1998). In this study, I deal with the first issue directly by limiting empirical observation to new businesses—those less than five years old at the time of incubation. I assume that most new businesses must address similar risks to failure and that incubation helps mitigate these risks. A better solution to the problem of modeling the start-up phase in an incubator would be to control carefully for the broad array of business support services that tenants of business incubators require and the services that business incubators are able to deliver. However, measuring the quality of these technical exchanges is beyond the scope of this research. An additional strategy for taking into account the idiosyncratic needs and differences between incubated new businesses is to control for two demographic attributes: gender and minority status. According to scholars, these two attributes reflect differences in motivation, experience, and access to resources of nascent entrepreneurs (Fairlie & Robb, 2008; Shane, 2008).

2.4.1 Dimensions of Business Incubators

The tremendous growth of business incubators across the U.S. and the local economic challenges that incubators are designed to address has resulted in a diversity of incubation practices. Incubators vary according to their type of incorporation, size, focus, and mixture of services.

Incorporation as a nonprofit or for-profit is a key demographic feature of incubators since most incubators require fiscal sponsorship in order to operate (Bartik, 2003). Typical sponsors and directors of incubators include federal, state, and local governments, chambers of commerce, industrial associations, nonprofit organizations, corporate and private investors, and universities (Cox, Daily *et al.*, 1991; Enright, 2003; Johnsrud, Theis, & Bezerra, 2003). At a minimum, the varying interests and oversight of these fiscal sponsors likely affect incubators' priorities regarding financial performance. For example, private and corporate investors expect a return on investment, while nonprofits and government agencies might not shy away from subsidizing operations as long as other outcomes are attained, such as a markedly increased local employment (Hedley, 1998). Sponsorship of a business incubator is also important because sponsors affect the governance and performance goals of an incubator. For example, a for-profit incubator pressed to generate profits might invest in new firms using developed technologies while an incubator sponsored by a university might support new firms developing innovations that lack markets or markets with low margins such as those in the developing world.

Incubators also differ in terms of their incubation and economic development strategies, which are closely associated with their goals and facilities. Incubator facilities can originate from abandoned manufacturing and office buildings, newly created research labs, or planned real estate development projects (Hackett & Dilts, 2004). Incubators with large facilities have the option to fill their vacant space with a single large tenant or break the space into smaller units to incubate multiple new businesses.

Incubators also differ in how and whom they choose to incubate. While many incubators consider themselves mixed-use facilities, meaning they do not specialize in helping businesses in a particular industry, it is also common for incubators to specialize. At the moment, 40% of existing incubators focus on technology oriented business, 30% are generalists, and the remainder focus on niche industries such as agriculture, arts, or services (Bartik, 2003).

The evolution of business incubators has generated several models of incubation and, as technologies and opportunities emerge, some incubators have adapted to meet these trends. New types of incubation occasionally spring up as well. For example, during the dot-com boom, several for-profit incubators emerged to support computer technology-based businesses (Halkides, 2001) and today new incubators are emerging to focus on clean energy businesses.

2.4.2 Key Findings on Business Incubation

Studies focused on the performance of tenants of business incubators are rare and often lack good designs. Many studies ignore tenant performance and focus instead on whether business incubators contribute to the overall economy in a community. Studies also exist which examine related programs such as technology transfer offices and treat incubation as a control measure (Di Gregorio & Shane, 2003).

Much of what is known about business incubation's effectiveness today comes from their trade association, the National Business Incubation Association (NBIA). According to the 1997 NBIA study *Business Incubation Works* (Molnar, 1997), 87% of tenants who graduate from an incubator survive the transition and 84% of these graduates remain in operation in the same community where they were incubated. This finding is often used to advocate that incubation is a practice that promotes endogenous economic growth as opposed to smokestack chasing where communities use lucrative incentives to lure corporations and manufacturers away from other communities (Bartik, 2005). NBIA's 1997 study also claims that for every \$1 invested in subsidies to business incubation, tenants and graduates of business incubators generate almost \$30 in local tax revenues (Molnar, 1997). This fact further supports the claim that incubators are a cost-effective way to increase local economic performance.

Despite NBIA's efforts to evaluate itself and its members, and its use of trained scholars in conducting research on the impact of business incubation, NBIA's research has been criticized for its lack of rigorous sampling methods (Bearse, 1998). The results of NBIA's 1997 study did not control for non-responses to its survey and much of the self-reporting from incubators is suspected to be inaccurate. In addition, the study relies on a non-random sample of 23 firms selected from a non-random sample of four incubators. However, the study broke ground in its efforts to address systematically the lack of knowledge about the impact of incubation on local economic growth and firm performance.

In the academic literature, research on business incubators began in the late 1980s when the industry was young. Most of this work often focused on describing the concept and reporting descriptive statistics on the population of incubators (Allen & McCluskey, 1990; Hackett & Dilts, 2004). In one of the first studies to use statistical analysis to estimate how attributes of incubators related to job creation and number of tenants graduated, Allen & McCluskey (1990) found that the age and size of an incubator were positively related to tenants' job growth and higher rates of graduation. This study was comprehensive in that it used a NBIA roster to survey all known incubators at the time and it achieved a 70.5% response rate, which the authors claim reflected a random distribution of the population. The study also attempted to control for various characteristics of incubators such as whether the incubator operated as a nonprofit or not and the types of services it offered, but the effects of these variables were not statistically significant. It is curious to note that even though a precedent to use statistical analysis to evaluate incubation practices dates to the 1980s, similar types of studies have not been repeated. Explanations for the lack of follow-up studies has centered on the difficulty of maintaining data-gathering processes for repeated statistical analyses (Hackett & Dilts, 2004).

Until recently, the only other U.S.-based study to attempt a similar type of analysis to Allen & McCluskey (1990) is one by Phillips (2002), which models the use of nonparametric methods to conduct evaluation of economic development programs. Because Phillips relies on a small sample and data collection did not assume a population distribution (Phillips, 2002), the study's findings are not generalizable. However, the study offers preliminary findings useful in designing robust empirical methods. In her study of tenants of the Advanced Technology Development Center (ATDC) in Atlanta, Georgia, Phillips (2002) conducted a test of the differences in means of various performance attributes of incubated and unincubated businesses. She found that mean rank differences were statistically significant in employment growth, financing access, labor access, and technology transfer (Phillips, 2002). Thus, the study concludes that several of the advantages that incubated businesses are supposed to receive from incubation services were in existence in this one case. The study also breaks new ground in methodology because of its use of a comparison group to assess differences in performance between incubated and unincubated businesses.

Most recently, a study sponsored by the U.S. Department of Commerce's Economic Development Administration (EDA) looked into whether its investments in local economic development infrastructure were associated with local employment growth trends (Arena, Adams, Noyes, Rhody, & Noonan, 2008). This study, conducted by the accounting firm Grant Thornton, uses data from the $311 million that the EDA invested between 1990 and 2005 in matching funds to support the construction of community, industrial, transportation, commercial, and business incubator facilities. The objective of this study was to investigate how public infrastructure funding from the EDA relates to permanent job creation in communities receiving EDA grants. The study specifically used regression analysis and a quasi-experimental method to compare job growth in counties receiving EDA funding with counties that had not received EDA funds. Overall, the study found that EDA funding was statistically significant and generated positive job growth in rural communities but not in urban settings. Furthermore, the study found that business incubator construction projects generated more job growth per dollar in funding than all other types of EDA construction grants. Thus, it is estimated that per $10,000 in EDA grant funding, business incubators generate 46.3 new jobs at a cost of $216 per job. In comparison, commercial development projects generated 9.6 new jobs per $10,000 at a cost of $1,008 per job. While the design of the study is sound and uses official U.S. government employment data, the study's worthiness is difficult to assess since official statistical results are not published. In addition, the study uses a measure of job growth that is not entirely adequate. While the study sought to measure permanent job creation as opposed to construction-related job growth, the implementation of the measure is suspect in that the authors did not remove construction-related jobs from the data. Instead, they addressed this problem by using a temporal measure of job growth that only measured employment after the 3rd year of a grant. They justify excluding measurements of employment during the first 3 years of grants, since the average construction project in the study lasted 3 years. Thus, the measure for permanent job creation remains biased by those projects whose construction time exceeded 3 years. Despite the flaws of the study, its findings have shed credibility on the effectiveness of business incubators in generating employment growth and its use of a quasi-experimental method is an improvement in research in this field.

2.5   Observations

This literature review covered four topics: defining the concept of entrepreneurship, explaining the role public policy plays in entrepreneurial activities, explaining business incubation programs, and summarizing key studies on the effectiveness of business incubators in generating local economic growth. This section sought to frame entrepreneurship as a phenomenon whose positive effect to society emerges when entrepreneurs engage in productive as opposed to unproductive entrepreneurial economic activities (Baumol, 1993). I made the case using Baumol's theory that entrepreneurship is a benefit to society when it generates a higher level of economic output as seen through increased supplies of goods and services as opposed to when it creates profits without increasing supplies (Baumol, 1993).

Baumol (1993) and Shane (2003) serve as an entry point for outlining the entrepreneurship process and a discussion of why government intervenes in entrepreneurial activities. The entrepreneurship process makes it clear that new businesses emerge from a sequence of events with multiple participants who engage in creating, discovering, and exploiting new opportunities and that opportunity motivates new business development. Governments, especially local governments, now play a larger role in helping create a context where individuals can engage in entrepreneurship through new business creation. A summary of key studies on policies intended to help individuals engage in entrepreneurial activities shows that some of these programs are marginally successful. More importantly, the summary of these studies reveals that more work needs to be done by scholars applying robust designs, gathering better data, and presenting findings transparently and thoroughly.

I aim to advance the good work begun in policy evaluation of entrepreneurship programs by focusing on business incubators. This study returns to the roots of incubator research by conducting a national study similar to Allen & McCluskey's (1990) and looking at attributes they attempted to control for, but found to be insignificant.

Chapter 3

Data Collection and Descriptive Statistics

> We have graduated 27 clients, resulting in 35 companies, and advised over 400 others. Typically it takes three to six years for a client to graduate, and that depends on whether they have certain federal regulations to hurdle. Existing clients and graduates have annual revenues in excess of $200 million with over 650 employees. Of our current clients, 60% are minorities, 20% are disabled vets, and 33% are women owned. It just happens that way... The Hampton Roads Technology Incubator System each year creates the following tax impacts: for Hampton Roads, $1.5 million; for the State of Virginia, $6 million; and for the federal government, $18 million. Yet our only investor is the City of Hampton. Fortunately, they are very forward thinking. We run the incubator on an annual budget of $185,000 when it usually takes around $400,000.
>
> — TIMOTHY EARLY, President & CEO, Hampton Roads Technology Council
> March 17, 2010 hearing of the House Committee on Small Business

Sufficient firm level data to conduct experimental research to investigate whether an incubated business benefitted from being incubated has eluded scholars for years (Hackett & Dilts, 2004). While data on successful incubated businesses is readily available, data on failed incubated firms is rarely publicized. Additionally, incubators do not collect data on comparable unincubated businesses (Hackett & Dilts, 2004). To overcome this lack of data, I found a reliable third-party source that contained a large sample of incubated and unincubated businesses. The incubated businesses were identified by matching their establishment address with known incubators' addresses. This study therefore relies on three unique datasets:

1. A panel of demographic information on business incubators;

2. A panel of all firms—for-profit, nonprofit, and government—operating at the same address as a business incubator, extracted from the National Establishment Time-Series Database (NETS); and

3. A second NETS panel of for-profit firms which were demographically similar to the for-profit firms that shared a business address with an incubator but which were located at a different address.

This chapter reviews how I assembled, processed, and prepared for analysis each dataset. Additionally, I present key descriptive statistics on business incubators, incubated businesses, and the matched control group of unincubated businesses.

3.1 Business Incubator Data

The panel of business incubator data consists of approximately 934 business incubators, which have been located in approximately 993 establishments[1]. In constructing this panel, I used several iterative steps to confirm all the known addresses of each incubator, its size in square feet, and whether it specialized in incubating specific types of firms, was incorporated as a nonprofit organization, or was affiliated with an institution of higher education. An explanation of how the population of business incubators was assembled and incubator data was collected follows.

---

[1] Note that the discrepancy between my population total of business incubators and the 1,600 incubators counted by the National Business Incubation Association (NBIA) is likely due to different definitions of incubation. NBIA counts as incubators and members several organizations that do not offer physical operating space and others that are in the process of being created.

Business Incubator Population

I created the most inclusive and exhaustive possible census of business incubators by collecting membership rosters from the National Business Incubation Association and 23 state associations of business incubators, plus economic development resource lists from 50 state governments and national rosters for the years 2007 and 2009 from the University of Central Florida Business Incubation Program.

To avoid overrepresentation of successful and younger incubators, Walls & Associates using the NETS conducted an additional search for incubators having closed since incorporation. Because approximately 30% of the organizations in the master list contained the term "incubator" in their name, a search was done using the term's root "incubat." This search identified an additional 130 business incubators, many of which had ceased operations.

Data on each incubator site was then gathered and verified using six redundant steps. First, the incubator's name, physical address, contact information, nonprofit status, university affiliation, industry focus, year of birth, and size in square feet were researched using the search engine Google (www.google.com). This first step usually identified the incubator's website, from which its most recent physical address and several of the demographic attributes listed above could be confirmed.

When the incubator did not publish all of the required demographic information on its website, I conducted a second type of search using the Internet Archive (www.archive.org). The Internet Archive stores over 150 billion screen shots of web pages dating back to 1996. By looking back in time at the web sites of business incubators, I successfully verified data already collected and often pieced together the remaining demographic information necessary for the study. Often this searching revealed previous physical addresses where the incubator had maintained offices.

When the prior two steps failed to yield the full set of variables being collected, I proceeded to search for incubators using additional sources. The third database I searched was the master file of the National Center for Charitable Statistics (NCCS). NCCS is a clearinghouse of data on the U.S. nonprofit sector and its database could verify an incubator's founding year, last known address (if the prior searches failed to uncover these details), and whether it was incorporated as a nonprofit.

Fourth, I searched the D&B Million Dollar Database published by Dun & Bradstreet. This database lists approximately 1.6 million organizations. Searches using this database were fruitful in uncovering information on the size in square feet of an incubator, its founding year, and its last known address.

Fifth, I turned to LexisNexis Academic and searched for news stories, SEC filings, and company descriptions of incubators. Because most incubators receive government support and are centerpieces of economic development programs in communities, I often found stories detailing their opening ceremonies, successful tenants, and funding awards. These stories helped fill in missing pieces regarding each incubator's founding year, size, nonprofit status, and location.

Finally, in cases where research using the previous five steps did not generate a full set of demographic data for an incubator, I surveyed each incubator for which an e-mail address was available. My questionnaire asked the incubator to verify its last known address, provide its founding date, and estimate its size in terms of square feet[2].

The final Incubator Master List contained one observation per incubator address with variables for birth, death, nonprofit/for-profit incorporation, affiliation with an institution of higher education, type of specialization, and square footage.

3.2   Tenant Firm-Level Data

The National Establishment Time-Series Database is a new longitudinal dataset that tracks more than 36.5 million business establishments' name, address, birth, re-

---

[2]Sample questionnaire listed as Appendix A.

locations, industry, employment, annual sales, and legal status on an annual basis beginning in 1990 (Walls, 2009). This database relies heavily on the Data Universal Numbering System (DUNS) utilized by the marketing and business information firm Dun & Bradstreet (D&B). Walls & Associates, the vendor of NETS, produces this unique and timely dataset by taking an annual snapshot of the Duns Marketing Information file and other archival files of Dun & Bradstreet and licenses the information for research purposes only.

3.2.1   Population Frame

D&B defines business establishments as a "business or industrial unit at a single physical location that produces or distributes goods or performs services" (Neumark, Zhang, & Wall, 2005). The business establishments followed by D&B are identified through over 100 million telephone surveys, legal and court filings, news services, public utilities, all U.S. States' Secretaries of State registries, company filings, and the U.S. Postal Service. Recognizing that many firms own or control more than one business establishment in more than one physical location, the NETS distinguishes whether the business establishment record belongs to one firm or a multi-establishment firm (Neumark, Zhang, & Wall, 2006). Hence, for each business establishment, NETS tracks whether the business is a standalone firm headquartered at that physical address, a branch or subsidiary of a multiple establishment firm headquartered elsewhere, or a multiple establishment firm headquartered at that physical address.

Using a query which matched the known physical addresses of the business incubator population with the physical addresses of over 36.5 million business establishments in the NETS, a data extract—"NETS Full"—of approximately 38,000 establishments was pulled[3]. In this file, each of these 38,000 establishments shared the same address as a business incubator at some point between 1990 and 2008.

---

[3]NETS Full is a wide form panel of business and incubator data with only the last known address of the incubator.

In order to capture the relocation patterns of both businesses and incubators, Walls & Associates pulled a second "NETS Moves" dataset detailing every historical address where each firm and incubator existed[4]. It is important to note that while the first NETS dataset provided longitudinal performance measures of all firms that were co-located with an incubator, it was not possible to tell whether those measures reflect the firm's performance before incubation, while in incubation, or post-incubation. The NETS Moves dataset made it possible to determine the year when incubators and firms moved to an address and when they moved out or expanded. The NETS Moves dataset contains 7,137 observations for 5,615 businesses and 131 incubators that moved or expanded between 1990 and 2008. Note that the addresses for the 131 incubators that had moved or expanded were also added to the search query that led to the full NETS extract.

3.2.2   Data Merging and Manipulation

Assembly of the final dataset for analysis required five steps, which reduced the initial sample of 38,000 potentially incubated businesses to approximately 19,000. Figures B.1 and B.2 provide an illustration of the merging process.

First, I matched the Incubator Master List with the NETS Moves datasets using the DUNS number[5]. This revealed an additional 131 locations where incubators had previously operated. By listing the moves chronologically, I created two variables indicating when the incubator moved in and out of a particular establishment. These observations from NETS Moves were appended to the Incubator Master List.

Second, I matched the Incubator Master List dataset with NETS Full using the DUNS number. All matched observations were removed from NETS Full, which created a dataset of businesses co-located with an incubator. In addition, the Incubator

---

[4]NETS Moves is long form panel of data for businesses and incubators with more than one known address in the NETS.

[5]DUNS numbers for all incubators that are independently incorporated were identified with a query from Walls & Associates based on the incubators' names and known addresses.

Master List now contained NETS variables for those incubators that were separately incorporated and had a unique DUNS number. The Incubator Master List was now a time-series dataset of all known incubators with corresponding current and former addresses.

I conducted a third match in order to identify all businesses whose last known address was not the last known address of the incubator because the firm had moved in and then out of the incubator's establishment. In this step, I matched the Incubator Master List with multiple addresses per incubator with the NETS Moves dataset, which includes multiple addresses per firm. I used a matchstring that consisted of the zip code and address for each unique address location in both datasets to do the matching. Just like in the match with the Incubator Master List, this match was done in order to create two variables indicating when a firm moved in or out of a location inhabited by an incubator. Additionally, this long form panel was transformed into a wide form panel and merged with the NETS Full dataset using the DUNS number.

The fourth merging step identified all of the firms in the NETS Full which had previously been incubated but were no longer in an incubator, as well as those still being incubated. I did this by matching the Incubator Master List with multiple addresses per incubator with the NETS Full dataset using a zip code and address matchstring. This resulted in a reduced dataset of 32,711 businesses which were co-located with an incubator.

The fifth and final step in generating a dataset of firms co-located with an incubator and likely to have been incubated involved several data cleaning techniques. First, I dropped all businesses incorporated as nonprofits and all those falling under SIC codes for government. Then I dropped all firms that had existed for longer than five years at the time that their associated incubator was born. In addition, firms with an initial employment of over 100 and those determined to be large corporations were dropped. Finally, I dropped all firms that emerged after an incubator had ceased operations or moved out of a location. This resulted in a reduced dataset of 20,266 firms that were co-located with an incubator and highly likely to have been tenants of the incubator.

To assess the accuracy of the address matching process in identifying all former and current tenants of business incubators, I conducted a data audit. A random sample of 65 incubators and their matched tenants (1,200 firms) was pulled from the remaining dataset. I surveyed all 65 incubators via e-mail, asking their managers to report which of the listed firms were current or former tenants. The survey generated a 49% response rate and revealed that 78% of the listed firms were current or former tenants[6].

3.3   Unincubated Control Group Firm Data

To investigate whether incubated businesses perform better due to incubation, I needed to rely on quasi-experimental methods for estimating average treatment effects (Rosenbaum, 2002). These methods are designed to avoid the problem of selection bias (Rosenbaum, 2002). Because it is impossible to simultaneously observe the outcome of the same firm both under incubation and without incubation, I used a matching procedure to identify a valid control group which allows for outcome comparison between incubated and unincubated businesses (Caliendo & Kopeinig, 2008). Due to the fact that in this study I could not use random assignment to develop a group of incubated businesses and a control group of unincubated firms, the matching procedure used assumes that matching treated and untreated units on observables results

---

[6]It should be noted that, through further investigation, I uncovered inaccuracies in the responses from incubators. In some cases, respondents did not accurately recall former clients, especially if the incubator was larger and older and the respondent was new to the incubator's staff. In other cases, responses were simply incorrect. In one case, a respondent reported that several listed businesses were not clients of the incubator, but upon calling one of the clients directly, I discovered that the firm was still operating within the incubator. In other cases, I found out through research using the Internet Archive that several businesses that were reported not to have been tenants of an incubator were actually listed as tenants on that incubator's website in prior years. Due to these errors in reporting, I suspect the accuracy of my matching strategy is actually higher than 78%.

in equivalent distributions of observed covariates among both groups (Rosenbaum, 2002).

The design and extraction of an equivalent group of unincubated businesses from the NETS required two steps. I designed a general first-stage matching process that would create a database reflecting the full universe of unincubated businesses contained within the NETS. This was necessary because I did not have unlimited access to the full universe of the NETS database in order to extract multiple samples under different assumptions of relevant observed covariates that could predict incubation. Candidates for matching were firms not incorporated as nonprofits and which never resided in one of the locations were incubators had existed.

In the first stage, each incubated business was matched to seven unincubated firms based on founding year, county, industry, and the gender of the entrepreneur. Due to the high dimensionality of some of the observed covariates (i.e. founding year, county codes, and industry) (Caliendo & Kopeinig, 2008), an exact one-to-one matching technique was ruled out because it would have resulted in many unmatched cases. Hence, I created 420 matching strata that represented the general founding years, county codes, industry, and entrepreneur's gender of the approximately 19,000 incubated businesses. These 420 strata reflected seven general geography codes, five ranges of founding years, six industry groups, and two gender categories. For each incubated business that fell into one of the 420 strata, seven randomly matched firms without replacement were pulled out of the NETS. This dataset represented the universe of unincubated businesses within the NETS, which were similar to the incubated businesses in terms of geography, founding year, industry, and gender of the entrepreneur.

Because not all matches for each incubated business were equivalent in terms of the four matching criteria, I conducted a second matching step that further refined the matching by selecting the three unincubated firms for each incubated business that were most alike. In order to indentify the three closest matches, I used a propensity score, defined as the probability of receiving treatment given observed covariates (Rosenbaum, 2002). The use of a propensity score to create a matched dataset helps overcome the problem of dimensionality within observed covariates that makes exact one-to-one matching difficult (Caliendo & Kopeinig, 2008)[7]. Also, the propensity score acts as a balancing score that adjusts the distribution of observed covariates between treated and control groups. Propensity score matching helps reduce bias in observational studies when nonrandom assignment to treatment is not possible. The key to propensity score validity is the assumption that matching treated and untreated units with similar probabilities of receiving treatment allows for direct comparison of outcomes. In other words, if one can estimate a model for determining treatment using observed traits of treated and untreated cases, then one can create valid comparison groups without randomization (Rosenbaum, 2002).

Hence, I calculated a propensity score for each incubated and unincubated business that took into account 50 state dummy variables, 1,048 county dummy variables, founding year, nine industry dummy variables, and two dummy variables for gender and racial identity of the entrepreneur. Based on the calculated propensity scores, each incubated business was matched to its three nearest unincubated neighbors with continuous replacement. Thus, in some cases, an unincubated firm is part of a control group for more than one incubated business.

In order to determine that incubated and unincubated businesses shared similar likelihoods of incubation, I compared the density and distribution of their scores using Figure B.3. Based on the low levels of overlap for propensity scores higher than 0.5, I decided to drop those cases from the analysis.

Furthermore, I conducted two tests to determine whether matching based on propensity scores had generated similar distributions of matching covariates for treated and untreated cases. Table B.1 presents the mean values of the observed matching

---

[7]Note that propensity score matching was deemed to risky to conduct by Walls & Associates since they had not implemented this method before.

variables prior to matching and post-matching, a t-test for their equality, and a percentage for the standardized bias due to their differences. After matching, if the t-test for equality of means is rejected and the standardized bias is over 5% for any matching variable, there is reason for concern that the propensity score matching process yielded poor results (Caliendo & Kopeinig, 2008). This is not the case with any of the matching variables employed in this study.

3.4   Descriptive Statistics on Business Incubators

Table B.2 ranks each state and the District of Columbia based a count of business incubator establishments. The ten U.S. states with the largest number of business incubators are California, New York, Texas, Florida, North Carolina, Ohio, Wisconsin, Georgia, Pennsylvania, and Virginia. California hosts almost 12% of all the business incubators in the nation, while New York, the state with the second largest number of incubators, hosts almost 8%. The fact that Massachusetts and Washington do not appear in the top ten is surprising given their national reputation as strong producers of high-tech industries.

Figure B.4 presents a histogram of the creation of business incubators by year and by nonprofit status. Prior to 1980, the population of business incubators had not reached 25; however, between 1980 and 2000, the business incubation industry grew steadily. The creation of business incubators peaked at almost 150 new incubators in 2000, which is attributable to a spike in for-profit and nonprofit business incubators as in seen in Figure B.4. However, the rapid ascent of for-profit business incubators in the turn of the century was unsustainable. Today, the majority of incubators are still incorporated as nonprofits; they represent 80% of the population and total 795 unique establishments in this dataset. In contrast to previous studies of for-profit incubators which estimate that they represent 10% of the incubator population (Linder, 2002), in this study I found that their numbers have grown and now represent 20% of the population with a total 198 establishments.

Figure B.5 presents a histogram of the creation of business incubators by year and by university sponsorship. University sponsored incubators total 264 or approximately 27% of the incubator population. Note that the growth in university sponsored incubators occurred mostly in the last decade and is likely tied to the growing role that universities and their technology transfer offices are playing in commercializing new technologies and in economic development. Additionally, university sponsored incubators span all levels of higher education, including community colleges, technical institutes, and for-profit colleges. Furthermore, university sponsored incubators do not focus solely on commercializing faculty research. Many of them also emphasize student-run businesses and offer space to local entrepreneurs.

Just like their tenants, incubators are also prone to failure. Figure B.6 is a histogram of business incubator failures by year. Beginning in 2000, incubator failures appear to follow the general trends of the national economy, with peak failures in 2002 and 2007. Additionally, for-profit incubators are more vulnerable to changing economic conditions. Figure B.7 shows that for-profit incubators fail more often in comparison to nonprofit incubators. In contrast, university sponsored incubators fail less often relative to non-university sponsored incubators, as seen in Figure B.8.

Table B.3 presents the average count of economic development, industry groups, and business support nonprofits and associations that are co-located with business incubators. The data shows that business incubators and their business trade and nonprofit peers are choosing to co-locate more often over time. Between 1990 and 2008, the number of business support nonprofits and associations co-located with an incubator has doubled.

3.5 Descriptive Statistics on Incubated Businesses

After cleaning and trimming the data, the final dataset of incubator tenants contains a total of 18,426 incubated businesses and 28,346 unincubated control group firms. Reflecting the growth of business incubation services, Table B.4 shows a steady increase in the number of business being incubated. The majority of incubator tenants were born after 2001. In addition, Table B.4 shows that 7,665 or approximately 42%, of incubated businesses failed. A large number of incubated businesses failed in 2004 and 2005, perhaps reflecting the lagged end of the dot-com boom. The timing of firm failures and the percentage of firm failures is similar in the control group, too.

Table B.5 presents a time-series of average initial sales for incubated businesses and the control group. Incubated businesses enter the market at a larger size. Their initial annual sales average $836,000, in comparison to the control group which averages $546,000. An anomaly in the data occurs in 1999, when the average incubated businesses started with sales of $2.4 million. I confirmed that for-profit software and technology incubators incubated the largest of these firms.

Table B.6 presents a time-series of average initial employment for incubated businesses and the control group. Incubated businesses enter the market at a larger size than their unincubated peers. They initially employ approximately 5 workers, in comparison to the control group that initially employs approximately 4 workers. However, looking at the minimum and maximum averages of initial employment between both groups reveals that their ranges are quite similar.

Most incubated businesses first begin operating inside an incubator. Table B.7 shows that 13,678 of the incubated businesses or approximately 72% of the sample, were born inside the incubator. A much smaller group of 5,338 firms first emerged in a location outside the incubator. Thus, it appears that most incubators recruit nascent entrepreneurs—individuals just beginning the business planning process—to fill their space, rather than seeking out fledging firms and enticing them to relocate.

A key benchmark that business incubators measure is their graduation rates. According to NBIA, business incubators should aim to have a tenant graduate from the incubator after 3 to 5 years of services. Table B.8 shows that, in fact, few incubated businesses ever leave an incubator. Out of 18,426 incubated businesses, only 3% or 527 firms exited the incubator. Of those 17% or 90 of the graduate firms failed after incubation. This indicates that incubators struggle to help their tenants build the capacity that they need in the amount of time being specified by the NBIA.

Looking at the relocation patterns of the two groups, it is noticeable that unincubated businesses relocate at a higher rate than their incubated counterparts. A total of 1,964 or 7% of the control group relocated during the period of observation. However, their rates of failure after relocation are similar to those of incubated businesses. Twenty percent of the control group firms that relocated failed subsequently.

One novel finding from Table B.8 is the large number of incubated businesses that left an incubator in 2007. While in most years an average of 28 incubated businesses graduate from an incubator, in 2007 a total of 247 incubated firms relocated to their own space. This is perhaps explained by the crash of the real estate market when operating space finally became affordable for these businesses. If this assumption is true, then it may be that an important reason why incubated businesses are not graduating is because they are too reliant on the subsidized space business incubators provide.

Table B.9 shows that business incubators primarily attract new ventures in the services sector. Service sector businesses represent almost 60% of the incubated sample. A much smaller group of incubated firms comes from the financial, insurance, and real estate services industries.

3.6   Conclusion

Overall, the collected data reveals that the performance of incubated businesses is highly correlated with the economic cycle. In periods of growth, incubated businesses begin with more employment and higher sales than their peers. However, incubation does not necessarily help firms avoid failure, nor does it prepare them to survive on their own. This is most notable from the data showing that only a miniscule number of firms in the sample ever left the incubator.

In addition, the data show that there has been rapid growth in the number of business incubators beginning in the mid-1990s. This growth occurred in two major spurts. First, during the dot com boom and then after 2000 when universities began expanding their technology transfer and economic development infrastructure.

In general, the data is national in scope and its collection occurred between 2007 and 2009 after the vast majority of incubators were formed. This leads me to conclude that the census succeeded in capturing the majority of business incubators. This is true of the population of incubators created after 1990 because it is after this period that the Dun & Bradstreet data is most reliable and when the electronic archival methods that I used are most appropriate.

Chapter 4

Does Incubation Lead to Higher Performance?

The heart of a true business incubation program is the ongoing, personalized, and comprehensive services that are provided to clients. By following best practices, an incubator will customize its mission, clients targeted, services provided, and infrastructure that is required in order to integrate its program into the fabric of the community and the broader economic development goals of the region. A best practice incubator will provide the expertise, networks, tools, and a social capital environment that will dramatically enhance the success of a new entrepreneurial venture. An incubator can become the catalyst for the creation of a business cluster in a community, county, state or region by creating concentrations of interconnected companies, suppliers, service providers and associated institutions.

— LOU COOPERHOUSE, Director, Rutgers Food Innovation Center
March 17, 2010 hearing of the House Committee on Small Business

For years, policymakers and economic development experts have lauded the scope and reach of business incubators—institutions that provide subsidized space and management support to new ventures. Having grown from 12 in 1980 to approximately 1,400 today, business incubators receive generous financing from government, investors, and universities who believe incubators will increase economic growth by nurturing good business ideas into profitable and growing firms. But do they? To date, little systematic knowledge exists about the value of incubation services to a new venture's competitiveness in the external environment.

New businesses could certainly use the help. Over half of new businesses fail in five years (Cressy, 2006), while profits for the typical surviving firm hover around $39,000 per year (Shane, 2008). Yet despite this lackluster performance, for the last 30 years local governments have shifted their economic development strategy away from retaining and attracting large incumbent firms (Bartik, Boehm, & Schlottmann, 2003) to encouraging individuals to start businesses that can exploit new opportunities and grow quickly (Pages, Freedman, & Von Bargen, 2003). Business incubators are one such strategy. In this chapter, I investigate whether business incubation helps new ventures survive and thrive in comparison to unincubated businesses.

This is an important line of empirical inquiry because incubation itself is theoretically questionable. Indeed, the assumed benefits of business incubators contradict the logic of market competition and evolutionary theory (Aldrich, 1999). Aldrich posits that the processes of firm selection and retention occur at two levels—internally within organizations and externally in the environment. While internal selection protects organizations from the pressures of the external environment, it can also stymie their ability to adapt to a competitive external environment. Hence, while incubation might insulate a firm from competitive forces of the external environment and increase its likelihood of short-term survival, incubation could also weaken the firm's ability to compete and survive once it leaves the incubator.

Although the study of incubation dates back to the 1980s, there is scarce quantitative empirical research that evaluates the effects of incubation on new venture performance. DiGregorio and Shane (2003) and Rothaermel and Thursby (2005) are among the few to apply statistical analysis to incubation performance questions. However, both of these studies omit control groups of unincubated new ventures and thus fail to address the important question of the relative advantages or disadvantages of incubation. Given the lack of robust research that examines the effects of incubation on new ventures, this study investigates whether incubated businesses outperform unincubated firms.

The data and design of this study follow the classic quasi-experimental model with a treatment group, matched control group, and longitudinal observations. I conducted analyses at the firm level using propensity score matching to estimate the average treatment effect of incubation in a sample of approximately 35,000 incubated and unincubated businesses. I estimated the average treatment effect in three ways—as sales growth, employment growth, and survival independently—while controlling for characteristics such as industry, the race and gender of the entrepreneur, and location and time fixed effects.

In the paper that follows, I first draw on the concept of liability of newness to explain how incubators help new ventures diminish risks that lead to failure due to their lack of market experience and legitimacy. This section outlines the logic behind why incubation is believed to help new ventures. I then discuss evolutionary theory to describe the possible long-term effects of incubation on new venture performance. I follow-up with a presentation of the data collected and the estimation techniques employed. I conclude with results of the study, along with limitations and future areas of research.

4.1 Business Incubation and the Liability of Newness

A business incubator is an organization that supports the creation and growth of new businesses by providing subsidized office space, shared administrative services, access to capital and financing, networking opportunities, and assistance with legal, technology transfer, and export procedures (Allen & Weinberg, 1988; Erlewine &

Gerl, 2004; Hackett & Dilts, 2004). The fact that 61.5% of new firms close within five years of founding motivates those who create business incubators and those who seek incubation services (Geroski, 1995). Local governments and policymakers support business incubation because they assume incubators can generate employment, innovation, and growth by helping new businesses avoid failure (Erlewine & Gerl, 2004). Likewise, new businesses seek incubation to access knowledge and assistance that will allow them to develop, test, and market new goods and services at a profit.

A key assumption that this study tests is whether business incubators help new firms overcome the liabilities of newness. When new firms enter a market, their survival often hinges on their ability to overcome three forms of novelty: market, production, and management (Shepherd, Douglas, & Shanley, 2000). Being new to a market, to production processes, and to management can hinder a firm's survival and growth until the firm establishes legitimacy, efficiencies, and organizational systems (Shepherd, Douglas et al., 2000) that enable it to maintain a flow of heterogeneous resources necessary for production and exchange (Nelson & Winter, 1982).

Novelty to the market describes the degree to which customers are familiar with a new venture (Shepherd, Douglas et al., 2000). When a firm enters a market, it faces a competitive disadvantage due to its lack of customer loyalty (Porter, 1980) and legitimacy as a viable provider of a valued product or service (Aldrich, 1999). Without a secured customer base and a viable product, new firms also lack the legitimacy necessary to secure financing crucial for establishing and growing operations (Aldrich, 1999). Novelty to the market is difficult to overcome both when a firm enters an already established industry and when it attempts to enter a completely new industry (Aldrich, 1999).

Novelty in production reflects the extent to which entrepreneurs are experienced with the technology and manufacturing processes used to deliver a product or service (Shepherd, Douglas et al., 2000). When entrepreneurs lack experience in the production processes being employed, costs of time and money may increase, especially if these processes rely on new or unproven technologies. Additionally, entrepreneurs may struggle with improving and discovering efficiencies in production processes if they are novel, which can delay the creation of economies of scale (Porter, 1980). Finally, the pressure to overcome novelty in production can create internal conflict in new ventures that leads to failure. This is especially the case in new ventures with dangerously low levels of resources. When innovation teams incur high levels of conflict, it has been shown that the ability to succeed at innovation dramatically falls (De Dreu, 2006).

Finally, novelty to management hinders new venture survival when the entrepreneur lacks adequate managerial skills, prior working experience with a start-up firm (Fairlie & Robb, 2008), or relevant industry experience (Shepherd, Douglas *et al.*, 2000). Because starting a new venture is risky, involves coping with uncertainties, and requires both generalist and specialized knowledge, new ventures can fail if entrepreneurs lack skills and abilities that can help them organize and manage a business. In fact, studies show that entrepreneurs who invest first in management and organizing activities generally succeed in raising the legitimacy of their business, which aids in securing resources (Delmar & Shane, 2004). Additionally, it is known that venture capitalists pay particular attention to the management experience of potential investment prospects and that they generally choose to invest in entrepreneurs with high levels of management experience (Shepherd, Douglas *et al.*, 2000). Furthermore, entrepreneurs who seek venture capital and are denied investments often attribute their lack of financing to their low quality and quantity of managerial experience (Shepherd, Douglas *et al.*, 2000).

Combined, a new firm's novelty to the market, to production, and to management impede its growth and threaten its survival (Porter, 1980). Because new entrants into a market might be undercapitalized, unknown, and inexperienced, they potentially face strong retaliation and price cutting from incumbents wishing to protect their market share and profits (Porter, 1980). Additionally, new ventures face internal challenges, such as generating production efficiencies and functional administrative processes that can cause them to fail. In order to help reduce these risks of failure, business incubators have emerged to help new ventures offset their lack of financial, technical, and management capacity. By offering free or subsidized space and management training, business incubators protect new ventures from the full forces of the external competitive environment and reduce barriers to market entry (Porter, 1980). Business incubators believe their services strengthen new ventures so that they can emerge from the incubator and compete successfully in their local economy (Erlewine & Gerl, 2004).

In sum, the services that incubators provide to new ventures essentially seek to lower their liability of newness. Specifically, businesses incubators appear to address most directly a firm's novelty in production and novelty to management. Business incubators often rely on a network of experienced business leaders and management consultants to mentor and train their tenants (Erlewine & Gerl, 2004). These experts exert strong pressure towards conformity with standard business practices and thus help new ventures establish legitimacy (Aldrich, 1999). Therefore, if incubators are truly successful in lowering firms' liability of newness by helping them address their novelty to management and production, one would expect new ventures to have increased survival rates and faster growth while in incubation.

However, incubation could also have a negative effect on firms' outcomes, especially when it comes to survival. Perhaps the experience necessary to overcome the liability of newness in production and management cannot be addressed through training once a business has formed. In such cases, survival and growth may depend more strongly on experience, the industry that the firm entered, or initial assets than on access to low rent and business training. Also, it could be that firms that seek incubation services do so because their owner is less experienced or the venture is highly risky in comparison to similar types of ventures that do not seek incubation support. In such cases, the effects of incubation may not be able to compensate for the effects of risk factors that a new venture is born with. Regardless, incubators and their supporters generally assume that incubation helps firms stay in business and grow faster even when taking into consideration the attributes of the owner and the firm.

4.2 Business Incubation and Organizational Evolutionary Theory

Unlike many organization and economic theories that ignore the forces that bring firms into being, organizational evolutionary theory seeks to describe the social, economic, and technological forces that give rise to new organizations and that change the nature of those organizations' functions and purpose over time. The perspective of this theory is longitudinal and thus makes its application to assessing the emergence, survival, and growth of new ventures relevant. Evolutionary theory describes four processes—variation, selection, retention, and struggle—to describe how populations of organizations emerge and vanish (Aldrich, 1999). In this chapter, I am particularly interested in testing assumptions regarding selection and retention of incubated businesses because determining whether incubation helps should entail demonstrating not only higher performance during incubation but higher performance post-incubation as well.

Variation occurs when individuals and organizations change their routines, competencies, or structural form (Aldrich, 1999). Such changes can be intentional and planned or can occur through luck or mistake. For example, when organizations invest in R&D they may create new production methods that improve on standard practices. This type of intentional variation contrasts with variations created blindly such as when organizations in moments of crisis resort to improvisation to mitigate losses. Improvisation in such a case may lead to discovery of new routines that improve on past organizational processes (Aldrich, 1999).

Not all created variations prove themselves useful to organizations, just like not all types of organizations prove themselves useful to the external environment (Hannan & Freeman, 1977). Thus, the utility of a variation to an organization depends highly on selection processes that grant certain variations legitimacy and resources for adoption. However, the selection process is theorized to be context dependent (Levinthal & March, 1993; Nelson & Winter, 1982). Because organizations exist in open environments, their preferences are influenced by the information and expertise that they gather from their surroundings (Nelson & Winter, 1982). Furthermore, organizations learn to cope with complex and multiple potential problems by simplifying their learning and accumulating knowledge inventories to respond to unpredictable and complex problems (Levinthal & March, 1993). Thus, what organizations learn from their environment and how they process this information for future reference is cyclical and bounded within the confines of physical space. Furthermore, once organizations learn to thrive in their limited and simplified context, they are prone to failure when that context changes (Levinthal & March, 1993).

Hence, selection in the context of incubation occurs in three sequential stages. First, incubators and prospective tenants must select one another. In evolutionary theory, the relationship between an incubator and a tenant is supposed to be symbiotic—the two parties exist for distinct purposes but their interdependence is mutually beneficial (Aldrich, 1999). Incubators depend on good tenants to demonstrate success and tenants receive not only survival-enhancing services but legitimacy in the external environment.

In the second stage of selection, incubators offer advice and help tenants select routines, competencies, and structures to improve their performance and odds of survival. However, selection assistance at this second stage may weaken the tenant in the long-run because it is making choices about its routines, competencies, and structure in an environment not fully congruent with the harsher and more competitive context that exists outside the incubator. Thus, while incubation may help firms survive in the long-run especially if the positive effects of incubation overcompensate for the innate weaknesses of a new firm, incubation could also have a negative effect once the firm is prepared to exist outside of the incubator environment.

In fact, evolutionary theory asserts that when organizations are "somewhat protected from their environments" they run the risk of permanent failure by developing competency traps that inhibit their ability to adapt to an externally competitive context (Aldrich, 1999). Thus, while incubation may help tenants overcome liabilities of newness, it can also impede new ventures from achieving complete independence if incubators lead tenants to select routines, competencies, and structures that are not viable outside the incubator. For example, the early advantages given to incubated businesses might lead entrepreneurs to believe that running a successful company is easier than it really it is when no assistance is being provided. Therefore, entrepreneurs may give less attention to addressing problems that the incubator by the nature of its services reduces.

The third stage of selection occurs outside the safe confines of the incubator and the process of organizational retention described in evolutionary theory determines its outcome. According to evolutionary theory, retention occurs when organizations are allowed to capture value from their selected variations (Aldrich, 1999). When environments retain organizations and allow them to secure resources and enact transactions with other individuals and organizations, the process of evolution has effectively made a choice in preserving, duplicating, and reproducing a specific set of routines, competencies, and organizational structures. The retained organizations—those that survive and hopefully grow—are the ones which have acquired a set of routines, competencies, and organizational structure that allows them to outcompete other organizations in the struggle for scarce financial and human resources, among others (Aldrich, 1999). The implication of this third stage of selection is that retained organizations are those that figured out how to operate efficiently and legitimately within a competitive environment for scarce resources.

Thus, evolutionary theory says, tenants will fail if there is a strong misalignment between the routines, competencies, and processes they develop in the incubator and those that unincubated ventures develop on their own. This happens because incubators and their tenants face different selection and retention pressures for their own survival than stand-alone businesses do. While incubators and tenants share the same competitive environment, they survive and thrive under different norms. Incubators, especially those in universities and nonprofit settings, do not compete in a for-profit context where organizational competencies for survival differ. Incubators survive partly due to their effectiveness in leveraging legitimacy with donors and policymakers who subsidize their operations, unlike for-profit firms which need to leverage marketing and production processes to sell goods and services. Thus, business mentorship of tenants by counselors who might not be deeply involved in running a for-profit business may lead incubated businesses to worse results.

Therefore, if incubation is truly a valuable service that enhances the survival and performance of new ventures, tenants post-incubation should not only survive but they should demonstrate higher overall performance than their unincubated counterparts. If incubated businesses survive at higher rates and demonstrate overall higher performance post-incubation than their unincubated peers, the finding would essentially demonstrate that incubated businesses have developed a superior set of routines, competencies, and structures that allow them to win in the competition for limited resources.

4.3   Data

To test the above hypotheses, I assembled and merged three datasets: a panel of the majority of business incubators operating in the U.S. between 1990 and 2008 and two panels of firm-level data from the National Establishment Time-Series Database (NETS) provided by Walls & Associates (Walls, 2009). Since incubators exist to help new businesses, I defined the unit of analysis as new businesses founded after 1989 and less than 5 years old at the time of incubation.

4.3.1   Business incubator data

The panel of business incubator data consists of 944 business incubators, which have operated in 1,121 locations. I used several online archival methods to confirm all known addresses of each incubator, along with its legal status, founding year, dissolution year if applicable, and affiliation with an institution of higher education[1].

I created the most inclusive and exhaustive possible census of business incubators by collecting membership rosters of the National Business Incubation Association, 23 state associations of business incubators, and economic development resource lists from 50 state governments. Because the majority of business incubators incorporate as nonprofit organizations, I also conducted a search for incubators using the master file database of the National Center for Charitable Statistics (NCCS), a clearinghouse of data on the U.S. nonprofit sector. In addition, I cross-referenced one national roster from the University of Central Florida Business Incubation Program for the year 2007.

To avoid overrepresentation of successful and younger incubators an additional search for incubators having closed since incorporation and those recently formed was conducted by Walls & Associates using the NETS. Because approximately 30% of the organizations in the master list contained the term "incubator" in their name,

---

[1]In special circumstances, where online research methods did not succeed in confirming all variables of interest for each incubator, I resorted to a short e-mail survey to acquire missing data, which garnered a 45% response rate.

a search was done using the term's root "incubat." The search identified an additional 130 business incubators, many of which had ceased operations.

4.3.2   Tenant firm data

Because data on failed incubated businesses is more difficult to find than data on successful incubated businesses (Hackett & Dilts, 2004), I extracted a sample of all incubated businesses from the NETS using address matching techniques. The NETS is a longitudinal dataset of over 36.5 million business establishments built from annual snapshots of Dun & Bradstreet (D&B) data (Walls, 2009). The NETS includes key geographic, descriptive, and performance data for businesses, such as every known address for a firm, the year in which a business moved into or out of particular address, industry codes, founding year, and annual sales and employment figures (Walls, 2009).

D&B defines business establishments as a "business or industrial unit at a single physical location that produces or distributes goods or performs services" (Neumark, Zhang, & Wall, 2005). This characteristic of the NETS database was crucial to conducting an address-based query to extract a population of likely incubated businesses. By matching the known physical addresses of the business incubator population with all current and former physical addresses of the 36.5 million businesses in the NETS, a data extract of approximately 38,000 likely incubated businesses was pulled.

4.3.3   Culling of tenant data

To finalize the incubator tenant population, several culling steps were required. First, firms founded prior to 1990 were eliminated because NETS does not provide annual performance data before that date. Then all businesses sharing an incubator's address but incorporated as nonprofits or falling under SIC codes for government were dropped. Because this study focuses only on the incubation of new and young businesses, I also dropped all firms that were over 5 years old at the time that their associated incubator was born. Firms with an initial employment of over 100 and those determined to be large corporations were also dropped[2]. Finally, all firms that were started at an incubator's address after that incubator had ceased operations were eliminated. These culling steps reduced the initial sample of 38,000 potentially incubated businesses to approximately 19,000.

To assess the accuracy of the address matching process in identifying all former and current tenants of business incubators, a data audit was conducted. A random sample of 65 incubators and their matched tenants (1,200 firms) was pulled from the remaining dataset. I then surveyed the 65 incubators via e-mail, asking their managers to report which of the listed firms were current or former tenants. The survey generated a 49% response rate and revealed that 78% of the listed firms were current or former tenants[3].

4.3.4   Unincubated control group

This study relies heavily on quasi-experimental methods for estimating the average treatment effect (Rosenbaum, 2002). These methods are designed to avoid the problem of selection bias (Rosenbaum, 2002). Because it is impossible to simultaneously

---

[2]Based on the definition of incubation and the entrepreneurship literature, I limit my sample to those firms deemed to be young and small-medium enterprises at the time of incubation. Thus, a young firm implies that the firm is under the age of 5 at the time it gets incubated. In addition, a small-medium enterprise restriction is used to exclude large public corporations from the analysis. For example, many incubators co-exist in business parks and commercial centers where multinational corporations also exist. I dropped out of the sample all firms which were clearly large corporations operating on their own but happening to share the same building and/or physical address as a business incubator.

[3]It should be noted that, through further investigation, I uncovered inaccuracies in the responses from incubators. In some cases, respondents did not recall accurately former clients, especially if the incubator was larger and older and the respondent was new to the incubator's staff. In other cases, responses were misleading. In one case, a respondent reported that several listed businesses were not clients of the incubator but upon calling one of the clients directly, I discovered that the firm was still operating within the incubator. In other cases, I found out through research using the Internet Archive that several businesses that were reported to not have been tenants of an incubator were actually listed as tenants on an incubator's website in prior years. Due to the errors in reporting, I suspect the accuracy of my matching strategy is actually higher than 78%.

observe the outcome of the same firm under incubation and without incubation, matching techniques were necessary to identify a valid control group which allows for outcome comparison between incubated businesses and unincubated firms (Caliendo & Kopeinig, 2008). A valid matching method is especially necessary when random assignment into treatment and control groups is not feasible. A key assumption made when using these methods is that matching treated and untreated units on observables results in equivalent distributions of observed covariates among both groups (Rosenbaum, 2002).

Therefore, the design and extraction of an unincubated group of firms from the NETS required two steps. Because I did not have unlimited access to the full universe of the NETS database in order to extract multiple samples under different assumptions of relevant observed covariates that could predict incubation, I needed to design a general first-stage matching process that would create a database reflecting the full universe of unincubated businesses contained within the NETS. Candidates for matching were firms that were not incorporated as nonprofits and which never resided in one of the 1,121 addresses were incubators had existed.

In the first stage, each incubated business was matched to approximately seven unincubated firms based on founding year, county, industry, and the gender of the entrepreneur. Due to the high dimensionality of some of the observed covariates (i.e. founding year, county codes, and industry) (Caliendo & Kopeinig, 2008), an exact one to one matching technique was ruled out because it would have resulted in many unmatched cases. Hence, I created 420 matching strata that represented the general founding years, county codes, industry, and entrepreneur's gender of the approximately 19,000 incubated businesses. These 420 strata reflected seven general geography codes, five ranges of founding years, six industry groups, and two gender categories. For each incubated business that fell into one of the 420 strata, seven randomly matched firms without replacement were pulled out of the NETS. This dataset represented the universe of unincubated firms within the NETS, which were similar to the incubated businesses in terms of geography, founding year, industry, and gender of the entrepreneur.

Because not all matches for each incubated business were equivalent in terms of the four matching criteria, I conducted a second matching step that further refined the matching by selecting the three unincubated firms for each incubated businesses that were most alike. In order to cull the three closest matches, I used a propensity score, defined as the probability of receiving treatment given observed covariates (Rosenbaum, 2002). The use of a propensity score to create a matched dataset helps overcome the problem of dimensionality within observed covariates that makes exact one to one matching difficult (Caliendo & Kopeinig, 2008)[4]. Also, the propensity score acts as a balancing score that adjusts the distribution of observed covariates between treated and control groups. Propensity score matching helps reduce bias in observational studies when nonrandom assignment to treatment is not possible. The validity of propensity score matching rests on the assumption that matching treated and untreated units with similar probabilities of receiving treatment allows for direct comparison of outcomes. In other words, if one can estimate a model for determining treatment using observed traits of treated and untreated cases, then one can create valid comparison groups without randomization (Rosenbaum, 2002).

Thus in the second stage of matching, I calculated a propensity score for each incubated and unincubated business in my dataset that took into account 50 state dummy variables, 1,048 county dummy variables, founding year, nine industry dummy variables, and two dummy variables for gender and racial identity of the entrepreneur. Based on the calculated propensity scores, each incubated business was matched to its three nearest unincubated neighbors with continuous replacement.

In order to determine that incubated and unincubated businesses shared similar

---

[4]Note that propensity score matching was deemed to risky to conduct by Walls & Associates since they had not implemented this method before.

likelihoods of incubation, I compared the density and distribution of their scores using a propensity score histogram (see Figure B.3). Based on the low levels of overlap for propensity scores higher than 0.5, I decided to drop those cases from the analysis.

Furthermore, I also conducted two tests to determine whether matching based on propensity scores had generated similar distributions of matching covariates for treated and untreated cases. Table B.1 presents the mean values of the observed matching variables prior to matching and post-matching, a t-test for their equality, and a percentage for the standardized bias due to their differences. After matching if the t-test for equality of means is rejected and the standardized bias is over 5% for any matching variable, there is reason for concern that the propensity score matching process yielded poor results (Caliendo & Kopeinig, 2008), which is not the case with any of the matching variables employed in the study.

4.4   Descriptive Statistics

Table B.10 presents descriptive statistics on incubated businesses and their unincubated peers after matching and trimming of observations. Looking first at matching variables, the typical founding year for both groups is 2000. At 0.5%, minority owned firms make up a miniscule percentage of all incubated businesses, while women owned firms make up 6.1% of incubated businesses. Looking at industry classifications, incubated businesses overwhelmingly compete in the services sector. 59% of incubated businesses fall in this sector, while the next highest group of incubated firms, 11%, competes in the finance and insurance industry. These figures reflect the general trend of entrepreneurs starting businesses in the professional and personal services sector (Shane, 2008).

In terms of age and survival trends, the average incubated firm stays in business for a total of 5 years and 42% of incubated businesses fail by the time they are 3.63

years old. This percentage of failure for incubated businesses is better than general estimates of firm failure which predict that 50% of new firms will fail within 2.5 years (Cressy, 2006).

Graduation rates are a key benchmark for business incubators. They reflect the ability of incubators to help their tenants achieve economic stability and overcome the liability of newness so that they can compete independently in the external environment. However, based on the data collected, incubators are failing in this respect. Only 4% of the sample or 655 incubated firms, managed to exit their incubator, over an 18-year period, having spent an average of 3.84 years in the incubator. Therefore, among the 18,426 incubated firms in the study, 7,543 of them failed while in incubation, 193 of them failed after incubation, 464 of the graduates remain in operations, and the remainder, 10,226, continue operating in the incubator. On average, an incubated firm spends 4.5 years in incubation.

Based on these observations, it appears that much of the success that incubators and policymakers claim is overstated. One possible explanation for my lower number of total incubated firms is that my census still left out many former and current incubators. In addition, the NETS only gathers information on businesses that have applied for a DUNS number. Perhaps the larger tenant figure from the business incubation industry includes a population of self-employed individuals who have not incorporated and applied for a DUNS number. Despite these potential drawbacks in the data, it still appears that incubators are not fulfilling their goal of preparing new ventures to survive and thrive outside the safety of the incubator.

Comparing sales figures between the incubated and control groups, incubated firms have higher sales. They average $693,000 in sales their first year in business in comparison to the control group which averages $437,000 in their first year in business. Overall, sales in both groups decline based on the first year that a firm achieved positive sales and the last year that a firm achieved positive sales. However, the decline is much larger for unincubated firms, which average a 3% decrease in sales annually in comparison to incubated firms, which average an 1.26% decrease. This implies that business incubators slow down the rate of demise for their tenants in comparison to the control group.

A comparison of employment figures between both groups reveals similar trends. Incubated firms are larger, with an average of 4.43 employees versus 3.45 employees for the control group. In terms of employment growth over time, incubated firms also outperform their counterparts. Incubated firms increase employment by 3% annually in cmoparison to the control group which averages 0.74% annual employment growth.

This review of the descriptive statistics point to the importance in controlling for the initial size of the firms since incubated firms tend to emerge as larger organizations. This larger size may be due to unobserved selection bias where incubators are selecting tenants with more resources initially. The differences in initial size between the two groups offers some evidence of possible lurking unobserved covariates and encourages use of estimation techniques that control for omitted variable bias and tests for the possibility of endogeneity of the treatment variable.

4.4.1 Performance Measures

I used three performance measures—survival, employment growth, and sales growth—which were selected for their theoretical and policy implications. Empirically, we know that new businesses are slow to grow and that firm survival is a stronger measure of firm performance when firms are young (Geroski, 1995). Yet, a strong motivation for why policymakers support entrepreneurship programs is the claim made by business incubators that they speed up the growth process, especially in regards to employment (Hackett & Dilts, 2004). On the other hand, entrepreneurs pay most attention to metrics like sales and revenue growth (Davidsson and Wiklund, 2006).

Following much of the firm growth literature which relies heavily on Gibrat's proportional growth model (Coad, 2007a; Sutton, 1997), I defined growth as the log difference in firm size,

$$\text{Growth}_{i,t} = \log(\text{SIZE}_{i,t}) - \log(\text{SIZE}_{i,t-1})$$

Thus, *sales growth* is the log difference between annual sales at time t and sales at time $t - 1$.[5] Similarly, employment figures were first log transformed and then differenced in order to calculate annual *employment growth*. *Firm failure* was measured by examining the last year in which a business was active in the NETS. Firm failure is a dummy variable equal to 1 if the last year of activity reported by the NETS is not 2008.

4.4.2 Theorized Explanatory Variables

Incubation

Incubation is a dummy variable that equals one for incubated firms in the years in which they happen to share the same address as an incubator.

Post-incubation

Post-incubation is a dummy variable that equals one for formerly incubated firms in the years after which they shared the same address as an incubator.

Standard Control Variables

I controlled for several firm level effects: *firm-size*, *firm-age*, and *industry*. In addition, in the survival function, I controlled for the gender identity and racial identity of the entrepreneur, which are two traits that have been shown to relate to the performance of new ventures (Fairlie & Robb, 2008). Because smaller firms tend to grow faster than larger firms, controlling for firm-size effects is important (Coad, 2007b). Therefore,

---

[5]Annual sales figures were first adjusted to 2008 dollars based on the consumer price index before being log transformed.

sales lag measures firm size when the dependent variable is *employment growth* and *employment lag* measures firm size when the dependent variable is *sales growth* or *firm survival*. Switching measures of firm size in relation to the dependent variable is necessary to avoid statistical bias due to autocorrelation when a lagged dependent variable is included in the model.

The age of the firm is measured in years. Eight SIC dummy codes were used to control for industry effects: agriculture, construction, manufacturing, transportation, wholesale trade, retail trade, finance, and services. In addition, year dummies were used to control for overall economic trends. Table B.10 lists descriptive statistics on all dependent and explanatory variables.

4.5 Estimation Procedures

Because I used three control matches for each incubated firm, data for the analysis of survival and growth models were weighted. Incubated firms received a proportional weight of 1 and unincubated firms were given a proportional weight of 0.333.

4.5.1 Survival Analysis

Survival analysis is commonly used when the time at risk for experiencing an outcome differs among subjects, while needing to control for various treatments and demographic characteristics (Wooldridge, 2002). In this study, firms differ in their time at risk because they are born in different years. I used a parametric model with a log-logistic distribution after testing several distributions for best fit. I chose an accelerated failure time (AFT) model with a log-logistic distribution because it had the largest log likelihood value and the lowest Akaike Information Criterion value (Cleves, Gould, Gutierrez, & Marchenko, 2008)[6]. I also decided to use a parametric

---

[6]Table B.11 presents a comparison of a basic treatment model under different distribution assumptions.

model as opposed to a proportional hazard model because assuming a distribution allows for full use of all observations and makes it possible to account for time-varying covariates (Cleves, Gould, *et al.*, 2008). Additionally, to control for unobserved heterogeneity among firms, I modified the survival function to account for frailty (Cleves, Gould, *et al.*, 2008).

Frailty models generalize the survival regression model by accounting for the presence of an unobserved multiplicative effect on the hazard function (Gutierrez, 2002, p. 23). The effect of frailty is assumed to have a unit mean and finite variance that is not estimated from the data and its purpose is to account for heterogeneity or random effects.

Thus, the AFT unshared-frailty regression model using a log-logistic distribution is given as (Cleves, Gould, *et al.*, 2008):

$$S_\theta(t_i|x_i) = [1 + \{\exp(-\beta_0 - x_i\beta_x)t_i\}^{1/\gamma}]^{-\theta i}$$

In this model, the dependent variable is time until firm failure. θ_i represents an individual's frailty. When θ_i is greater than 1, that individual is considered "more frail for reasons left unexplained" by observed covariates and thus exhibit a higher risk of failure (Gutierrez, 2002). The fact that θ_i represents an unobserved multiplicative effect after accounting for observed covariates indicates that it mirrors the cumulative effect of omitted variables (Gutierrez, 2002).

The constant, β_0, represents the baseline hazard which, in its exponentiated form, signals whether the risk of failure is increasing if $\mathbf{e}^{\beta_0} < 1$ or decreasing if $\mathbf{e}^{\beta_0} > 1$. β_x represents the vector of coefficients that are to be estimated (Cleves, Gould, *et al.*, 2008). $1/\gamma$ represents a scale parameter with the specified log-logistic distribution. In the above model, $x_i\beta_x$ represents the following terms, which are similar as in the sales and employment growth models.

$$t_i|\theta_i = \quad \beta_0 + \beta_1 incubation_{i,t} + \beta_2 post\text{-}incubation_{i,t} + \beta_3 lag\ size_{i,t} +$$

$$\beta_4 firm\ age_{i,t} + \beta_5 women\ owned_{i,t} + \beta_6 minority\ owned_{i,t} +$$

$$\beta_{7-15} industry_{i,t} + \beta_{16-65} state\ dummy_{i,t}$$

4.5.2 Sales and Employment Growth

Panel data analysis is often used for policy evaluation because it has been shown to reduce statistical bias due to omitted variables and unobserved, time-constant factors that affect the dependent variable and are correlated with explanatory variables (Wooldridge, 2006). However, in the case of dynamic growth models where a future value of growth is partially dependent on a current value of growth, it becomes important to adapt panel methods to address issues of endogeneity, serial autocorrelation, and heteroscedasticity. Additionally, the chosen model must address the potential problem of treatment selection bias. Despite having used a propensity score matching technique to generate equivalent distributions between incubated and unincubated firms, my review of descriptive statistics signals potential bias due to incubation assignment being determined by unobserved covariates.

To address the problem of treatment selection bias, I chose to use a double difference model, which allows for the existence of unobserved heterogeneity being present in the process that leads firms to receive incubation services. As discussed when reviewing descriptive statistics, incubated firms differ in their initial size in comparison to the control group. This indicates that incubated firms likely hold more assets and differ in important unobserved characteristics, such as the entrepreneur's experience, education, and age. A double difference model should diminish the bias of unobserved heterogeneity as long as the unobserved traits that lead some firms to incubation are time invariant (Khandker, Koolwal, & Samad, 2009)[7]. Because time invariant differences get differenced away with panel fixed effects or first differences models, their bias can be eliminated.

Additionally, model specification of firm growth models tend to include lagged dependent variables. In order to resolve problems with endogeneity, serial autocorrelation, and heteroscedasticity that are introduced by lagging a dependent variable, I chose to use the Arellano-Bond system GMM estimator in Stata (Roodman, 2006). While a fixed effects or a first-difference estimator can solve the problem of potential selection bias due to unobserved omitted variables that predetermine treatment, these methods do not address autocorrelation and endogeneity due to inclusion of lagged dependent variables (Roodman, 2006).

In cases where one lacks a proper excluded instrument for the lagged dependent variable, an estimator with appropriate internal instruments from within the data can overcome the autocorrelation problem (Roodman, 2006). By using either the levels of $growth\ rate_{i,t-1}$ at $t-2$ and beyond or $\Delta growth\ rate_{i,t-1}$ at $t-2$ and beyond in a GMM framework, it is possible to estimate the double difference equation above, since lags 2 and beyond of $growth\ rate_{i,t-1}$ are orthogonal to $\Delta \epsilon_{i,t}$. To implement the Arellano-Bond system GMM estimator in Stata, I used the user written command xtabond2 for Stata (Roodman, 2006). The estimated model is the following:

$$\Delta growth\ rate_{i,t} = \beta_{0i,t} + \gamma_1 \Delta growth\ rate_{i,t-1} + \beta_2 \Delta incubation_{i,t} +$$

$$\beta_3 \Delta post\text{-}incubation_{i,t} + \beta_4 \Delta lag\ size_{i,t} + \beta_5 \Delta firm\ age_{i,t} + \Delta \epsilon_{i,t}$$

---

[7]Note that I did test the treatment variable for endogeneity using the two-stage regression methods described by Wooldridge (2002) with instruments by state that indicated if a state government had enacted a business incubation policy, a small business loans program, and/or a state sponsored venture capital fund. In the first stage results, the F-test statistic for the combined significance of the policy instruments was 11.25 revealing that they sufficiently estimated treatment. Furthermore, in the second stage, the F-test statistics did not reveal the treatment variable to be endogenous. However, the differences between pre-treatment outcome variables, which cannot be used for matching, still signal concerns with potential bias selection problems after matching.

4.6   Hypotheses

Based on the previously discussed theories of liability of newness and organizational evolution, I tested two hypotheses with the above survival, sales growth, and employment growth models.

> **Hypothesis 1:** Incubated new businesses will perform at higher levels than equivalent unincubated new businesses, indicating incubation helps overcome the liability of newness.

> **Hypothesis 2:** Incubated firms will outperform their counterparts post-incubation, indicating incubation helps firms adapt to the external environment.

4.7   Results

4.7.1   Effect of incubation on the hazard of firm failure

Table B.12 presents two separate estimates with exponentiated coefficients of the effect of incubation on the likelihood to fail. Model 1 represents the base model without controlling for *incubation* and *post-incubation* status of firms and shows that control variables behave similarly once *incubation* and *post-incubation* status is controlled jointly. Note that in a AFT regression, the estimated coefficient relates proportionate changes in survival time to a unit change in a given covariate (Jenkins, 2005). Thus, when the coefficient is less than 1 and a covariate increases by 1, the effect of the variable is to reduce survival time by $1 - \beta_x$ percent. Alternatively, when the coefficient is more than 1 and a covariate increases by 1, the effect of the variable is to increase survival time by $1 - \beta_x$ percent.

Focusing on Model 2 which accounts for the effect of *incubation* and *post-incubation*, results reveal that when firms enter incubation their expected time to failure decreases by 2%. In other words, incubated firms can be expected to go out of business sooner than their unincubated counterparts. Thus, based on this measurement, evidence exists refuting hypothesis 1 and reveals that incubation does not help reduce the liability of newness.

Furthermore, based on the significance and the larger effect of the *post-incubation* variable, the data show that once incubated firms graduate out of an incubator that their expected time to failure decreases further. Incubated firms that leave an incubator fail 10% sooner than their unincubated counterparts. This finding implies that incubation does not help firms develop a stronger set of routines, competencies, and organizational structures to compete in the external environment. Instead, the protective environment of an incubator appears to inhibit firms from developing the appropriate attributes to succeed in the external environment.

Examining the other control variables, there is nothing surprising about the effects of *employment lag*, a measure of firm size, and *firm age*. Many empirical studies tend to find that the risk of firm failure decreases firms grow in size and age (Geroski, 1995). The effect of *minority owned* also follows similar trends in the literature (Fairlie & Robb, 2008). A notable effect is that of *women owned*. While past research tends to show that new women owned firms fail sooner than new men owned firms, these results show that women owned incubated firms are less likely to fail than their male counterparts.

4.7.2   Effect of incubation on employment growth

Table B.13 presents the estimates of the effect of *incubation* on *employment growth*. A global F-test of estimated parameters for each model indicated that at least one of the estimated parameters was linearly associated with *employment growth*. Furthermore, the p-value for the AR(2) test statistic indicates that the instruments used in the Arellano-Bond system GMM estimator resolved the problem of autocorrelation, while the p-value for the Hansen statistic indicates that the model is properly identified. In both growth models, an increase of x units in a covariate leads to a proportional increase in percentage points on growth of $x \times \beta_x$.

In contrast to the survival models, the employment growth model 2 reveals that when firms enter an incubator their overall employment growth increases by 3.5 percentage points. This finding gives support to hypothesis 1 and indicates that incubation helps firms overcome the liability of newness by securing resources that enable them to grow at a faster rate than had they not been incubated.

In addition, the size and statistical significance of the *post-incubation* variable reveals that once a firm exits an incubator it is poised to grow further. Upon exiting an incubator, firms in this study increased their employment growth rate by 6.7 percentage points. Thus, this finding gives evidence to hypothesis 2 and shows that if we measure performance in terms of employment growth then incubation does enable firms to develop stronger capacities to compete and grow in the external environment.

Employment growth lag, sales lag, and *firm-age* behave as other empirical studies have shown them to perform (Coad, 2007b; Geroski, 1995). *Employment growth lag* is not significant but its negative sign indicates that large growth in the previous year reduces growth in the following year. *Sales lag*, which measures size of the firm, indicates that the larger the firm the lower its future growth change which Gilbrat's proportional growth theory helps explain (Geroski, 1995; Harrison, 2004; Sutton, 1997)[8]. *Firm-age* is not significant, positive but of small size.

---

[8]Gilbrat's proportional growth models assume that future size of firms is independent of current size. Thus, when the coefficient for firm size (i.e. *sales lag*) in the employment growth model is significant and not close to 1, it implies that firm growth does depend on size. In cases where the coefficient is less than 1 it signals that smaller firms tend to grow faster than their larger counterparts, which makes sense given how much more growth a larger firm needs to have an equivalent growth rate to a smaller firm.

4.7.3   Effect of incubation on sales growth

Table B.14 presents the estimates of the effect of *incubation* on *sales growth*. A global F-test of all estimated parameters for each model indicated that at least one of the estimated parameters was linearly associated with *sales growth*. Also, the AR(2) test statistic and the Hansen J statistic indicate that the Arellano-Bond system GMM estimator resolved the problem of autocorrelation and the model is properly identified.

Similar to the employment growth results, the sales growth models reveal that when firms enter an incubator their overall sales growth rate increases by 2.15 percentage points. This finding gives support to hypothesis 1 and indicates that incubation helps firms overcome the liability of newness by securing revenues that enable them to grow at a faster rate than had they not been incubated.

In addition, the size and statistical significance of the *post-incubation* variable reveals that once a firm exits an incubator that it is poised to grow further. Upon exiting an incubator, firms in this study increased their sales growth rate by almost 5.1 percentage points. Thus, this finding gives evidence to hypothesis 2 and shows that if we measure performance in terms of sales, incubation does enable firms to compete for and extract more financial resources from a competitive market.

The behavior of *sales growth lag, employment lag,* and *firm-age* reflect similar trends in the literature (Coad, 2007b; Geroski, 1995). *Sales growth lag* is significant and its negative sign indicates that large growth in the previous year reduces growth in the following year. *Employment lag,* a measure of firm size, is significant and indicates that the larger the firm the lower its future growth change (Geroski, 1995). *Firm-age* is not significant, negative but of small size.

4.8   Assessment of Results

In general, the findings from the three models measuring the outcomes of incubated firms signal that incubation helps new ventures grow faster in terms of employment and sales. However, what is the overall macro-economic effect of incubation on sales and employment growth given that incubated firms are expected to stay in business for a shorter lifespan?

Table B.15 presents predicted trends in survival, annual employment, and annual sales for four distinct groups: the control group, all incubated firms, incubated non-graduate firms, and incubated graduate firms. I assume that firms in each group start with an average of 4 employees and $250,000 in sales. I base survival probabilities for each group on the annual average predicted survival probability using Model 2 in Table B.12. To estimate annual employment, I first predicted annual employment growth for the study's sample using Model 2 in Table B.13. I then calculated the average employment growth rate for each distinct group. Thus, average annual employment growth among the group of graduate firms for example, takes into account both the period when those firms were in incubation and the period post-incubation. Finally, I compounded total employment based on the group's estimated average employment growth rate and the corresponding probability of survival. Total sales was calculated similarly.

Comparing, the average incubation effect with the control group's results, it is evident that after 10 years incubation dampens total employment and total sales losses but not firm closures. The surviving incubated businesses have lost 167 jobs in comparison with the control group's loss of 186 jobs. In other words, incubation helps incubated businesses save 19 jobs that would otherwise be lost due to the lower rates of employment growth for unincubated firms.

The predictions show that the effect of incubation on overall sales follow a similar trend. The incubated group's loss in sales is $1.2 million less than the loss in sales for the control group. After 10 years, annual sales among incubated businesses decline by $14.6 million in comparison with unincubated firms whose sales decline by $15.8

million. Based on employment and sales performance, incubation generally has a positive economic effect but it does not contribute to net economic gains since overall there are net losses in employment and sales for the incubated group.

Table B.15 also reveals that over 10 years the population of incubated firms decreases more in absolute terms compared to the control group. The loss is even higher for the group of firms that graduate from the business incubator. While the employment and sales growth models predicted that incubated firms that graduate from an incubator gain additional percentage points in growth, the survival model predicted that this group would die off sooner than had it remained in incubation. Looking at the average incubation effect for graduates, it is evident that the larger predicted sales and employment growth rates for graduates are not enough to compensate for their increased failure rates due to graduation. The losses in total sales for graduates is larger than the losses in total sales for the non-graduates. More striking are the losses in total employment for the group of graduates. Their loss in employment is even larger than the control group's signaling that incubated firms that graduate from an incubator are worse off than had they never been incubated.

This analysis of predicted trends in survival, employment, and sales reveals that incubation stems a firm's economic loss in terms of employment and sales but that it does not contribute positively to economic growth. Firms in incubation are better off than had they not been incubated but they are still more likely to fail and not grow. What could explain these results?

One explanation may lie in the signaling and guidance that incubated firms receive. Once a firm gets incubated, an incubator's close monitoring of the performance and changing competencies of its clients may generate information that leads incubated firms which are least likely to survive in the long-run to dissolve sooner. Therefore, the accelerated failure rates for incubated firms and the effect of this failure on net gains in employment and sales may be due to an incubator's ability to weed out failing businesses in the economy much sooner than the market would. Given that incubation subsidizes operations and management training, the economist Baumol (1993) would label this effect as productive entrepreneurship since incubation leads to savings of resources that would otherwise go to production that is not efficient and rent seeking.

Alternatively, these results may indicate that business incubators are poor judges of future business performance. While surviving incubated firms do grow and growth can be explained by the cost savings of incubation, incubators fail to identify and incubate firms most likely to survive. Among the incubated, incubators are selecting more often firms likely to fail than firms more likely to survive.

A final explanation for these results centers on the predictions of organizational evolutionary theory. Because incubated businesses learn to operate in an environment that is buffered from the full forces of the external environment, they do not learn how to thrive in the more competitive external economy. While incubation helps firms grow, this growth may lead firms to assume wrongly that they are competitive since their growth is tied to subsidies of costs and management training. Thus, incubated businesses may develop incongruous competitive behaviors that rely on the help of incubation while ignoring that the market may not accept or tolerate such type of competition in the long-run.

Understanding what drives these nuanced relationships between incubation, economic growth, and firm failure requires further study. Future research should seek to study closely the financial statements of a matched sample of incubated and un-incubated firms to determine how changes in costs and employment are correlated with changes in sales and profit. Acquiring such data would require implementation of rigorous survey methods or use of proprietary government databases such as the Integrated Longitudinal Business Database: Data Overview of the Census Bureau's Center for Economic Studies. This kind of research may help determine whether incubated businesses develop competitive behaviors that are unsustainable or if incubators are ignoring important indicators of future success when selecting tenants.

Alternatively, qualitative research on incubated businesses can explore whether incubation actually leads to productive entrepreneurship by accelerating the closure of unproductive businesses. Interviewing failed incubated businesses can help assess the quality of incubation services and identify mistakes that firms make while in incubation that lead to their demise. Additionally, interviewing incubated businesses regardless of failure could help probe whether selection bias exists in this study and generate ideas for how to better control for such a possible threat to validity.

Furthermore, qualitative research could help probe other predictions of evolutionary theory. Incubators often claim that they offer more than just space and that their services are more valuable because they provide important training and expertise in management and business development. Yet, these results indicate that incubated businesses make strategic mistakes in how they manage resources while in incubation and post-incubation. Perhaps because incubation subsidizes space and lowers the costs of administration through shared administrative services, incubated firms develop inefficiencies in how they manage their staffs to perform all the necessary functions that the business will need to perform once they exit the incubator. A study on how incubated firms respond to the type of counseling and training that incubators deliver may reveal potential problems in how incubated firms view incubation services and how incubators view their tenants.

4.9   Conclusion

For years, scholars have sought to know whether incubation has a discernable positive effect in the performance of their clients, while business incubators and policymakers have generally made claims that incubation is an effective service that helps firms survive and grow. This study used some of the best publicly available data, manipulated it using sound assumptions, and estimated the impact of incubation with robust estimation techniques. The findings reveal that the effects of incubation are potentially deleterious to the long-term survival and performance of new ventures. Incubated firms outperform their peers in terms of employment and sales growth but fail sooner. These are important findings for policymakers who support incubation as a strategy to increase employment locally and for entrepreneurs who risk their livelihoods in order to earn a decent living.

However, claims that incubators are highly successful and serve a significant number of businesses are overstated. The comprehensive process used in this study to identify the largest possible sample of incubated firms uncovered a fraction of the number of incubated ventures that supporters of incubation claim exist. While improvements are likely possible to the methods used in this study, this study roundly refutes the poorly documented and unpublished studies that cite much larger numbers of incubated firms and much higher levels of performance.

The methods and findings of this study showcase that more research is necessary to fully understand the effectiveness of incubation programs. Until then, these findings are instructive in helping and motivating business incubators to improve their past performance.

Chapter 5

Which Business Incubators Generate the Highest Levels of Economic Performance?

Historically there have been quite a few mixed use incubators that provide a variety of services to a diversity of industry sectors...In fact, [we are] now seeing more and more specialization; whether the sector is life science, telecommunications, biotechnology, food and agriculture or, particularly today, environmental technologies. The advantages of focusing on a specific sector are that we can provide much more specific services to clientele...We can also provide a cluster opportunity to really aggregate all of the elements of a particular industry together, the whole value chain, as well as aggregate resources that could provide the expertise that is needed, whether it is business marketing, production development, quality assurance, technology, and so forth to really meet the need of small businesses.

— Lou Cooperhouse, Director, Rutgers Food Innovation Center
March 17, 2010 hearing of the House Committee on Small Business

Starting a business is typically a risky and unprofitable endeavor. Over half of new businesses fail in five years (Cressy, 2006), while profits for the typical surviving firm hover around $39,000 per year (Shane, 2008). Despite the lackluster performance of the average new business, local governments for the last 30 years have shifted their economic development approaches from a focus on retaining and attracting large incumbent firms (Bartik, Boehm, & Schlottmann, 2003) to encouraging individuals to start businesses that can exploit new opportunities and grow quickly (Pages, Freedman, & Von Bargen, 2003).

Among the various programs devised to spur local economic growth, business incubation is now ubiquitous in local policies intended to bolster entrepreneurship at the local level. According to the National Business Incubation Association (NBIA), the number of incubators nationally grew from 12 in 1980 to over 1,400 in 2006. Incubators attract policymakers' support because of their promises to increase employment, innovation, and growth in distressed communities by helping new businesses avoid challenges that lead to failure (Erlewine & Gerl, 2004). Those interested in incubation include governments, nonprofits, universities, and private investors. They support incubation because of its promise to create economic value that communities can retain when new businesses are sheltered from the daunting challenges that many start-ups face (Erlewine & Gerl, 2004). But are they wise to do so?

Given that little systematic knowledge exists detailing whether incubators work (Hackett & Dilts, 2004), in this chapter I begin to examine whether particular models and strategies of incubation are more successful than others. The study uses a longitudinal dataset to probe whether the profit motives, knowledge resources, and network densities of incubators play a role in the performance of incubated firms. Since researchers lack consensus on how new businesses influence local economic growth (Fritsch, 2007), this study uses three measures of firm performance—survival, employment growth, and sales growth. By using a longitudinal dataset on incubators, incubated firms, and multiple measures of firm performance, this study begins to examine what drives successful incubation programs.

This chapter investigates whether traits of business incubators are associated with higher performance among incubated firms. I first frame the practice of business incubation in management and entrepreneurship theory in order to understand what motivates incubation. Because incubators assume a link between new business performance and economic growth, I present a summary of the state of research in these two areas. I then develop hypotheses on how the traits of incubators affect the performance of their tenants. I then proceed to describe the data, measurements, and analytical methods employed. I conclude by reporting results, offering an interpretation, and suggesting new avenues for research.

5.1   Business Incubation Policy

A starting point in this study are theories suggesting that new economic growth results from locally produced knowledge whose economic value is most easily exploited by those with close proximity to the source (Audretsch, Keilbach, & Lehmann, 2006). Additionally, research (Geroski, 1995) and theory (Baum, 1996) indicates that new businesses face a size and age disadvantage that leads to failure and stagnant growth in comparison to incumbent firms. As the U.S. transitions from an industrial economy to a knowledge-based entrepreneurial economy, a need exists to create new types of incentives and policies to spur entrepreneurship (Audretsch, Keilbach *et al.*, 2006). Incubators, which serve new businesses by facilitating knowledge transfer through networks and face-to-face consulting (Erlewine & Gerl, 2004), appear to pursue a new economic growth model; however, their efficacy is unproven.

5.1.1   Rationale for Incubation Policy

A business incubator is an organization that supports the creation and growth of new businesses by providing subsidized office space, shared administrative services, access to capital and financing, networking opportunities, and assistance with legal, technology transfer, and export procedures (Allen & Weinberg, 1988; Erlewine & Gerl, 2004; Hackett & Dilts, 2004). The fact that 61.5% of new firms close within five years of founding motivates those who create business incubators and those who seek incubation services (Geroski, 1995). Local governments and policymakers support business incubation because they assume incubators can generate employment, innovation, and growth by helping new businesses avoid failure (Erlewine & Gerl, 2004). Likewise, new businesses seek incubation to access knowledge and assistance that will allow them to develop, test, and market new goods and services at a profit.

Theoretically, competitive strategy and knowledge spillover perspectives can explain the rise of incubation programs and policies. From a competitive strategy perspective, new businesses face significant barriers to entry that impede their founding and threaten their survival once founded (Porter, 1980). Types of barriers to entry include the lack of economies of scale, capital requirements, poor access to favorable distribution channels, customer loyalty, cost disadvantages, and government regulations (Porter, 1980). Because new entrants into an industry might be undercapitalized, unknown, and inexperienced, they potentially face strong retaliation and price cutting from incumbents wishing to protect their market share and profits (Porter, 1980). The fact that new businesses lack several financial, technical, and management advantages that weaken their ability to compete against incumbents at the outset helps explain the emergence of incubators. Incubators help new firms organize routines that maintain a flow of heterogeneous resources necessary for production and exchange (Nelson & Winter, 1982).

Another explanation for the practice of business incubation comes from the knowledge spillover theory of entrepreneurship by Audretsch, Keilbach, & Lehmann (2006) which posits two locational factors that influence entrepreneurial activity. First, they argue that proximity to sources of knowledge production enhances entrepreneurial activity because economically valuable knowledge is often tacit and most easily transmitted through frequent face-to-face interaction (Audretsch *et al.*, 2006). A second factor—one that motivates many of the activities of incubators—stems from the need for communities to lower barriers to entrepreneurship. These barriers include creating incentives for knowledge production, increasing social network densities, reducing biases to failure, and influencing career choices (Audretsch, Keilbach *et al.*, 2006). These four factors have been shown empirically in economic research to be associated with entrepreneurial growth (Audretsch, Keilbach *et al.*, 2006). Because business incubators often collaborate with or are sponsored by research institutions (Markman, Phan, Balkin, & Gianiodis, 2005) and work with local business associations to motivate nascent entrepreneurs, they play a key role in addressing the market failures illustrated in knowledge spillover theory. In this chapter, I specifically look at how an incubator's university sponsorship and business association networks are related to tenant performance.

Whether incubators play a productive role in entrepreneurship (Baumol, 1993) and economic growth is an interesting empirical question. On the one hand, business incubators play the role of advocates for small and new businesses. They seek to transfer knowledge about business practices, culture, and competitiveness to new entrants that can potentially disrupt the economic playing field if their clients can grow quickly and become self-sustaining. This is especially true when incubators help launch new businesses in emerging industries or those using new technologies. On the other hand, business incubators may be promoting unproductive entrepreneurship if their practices shelter inefficient businesses from competitive forces. This study contributes to the literature on entrepreneurship policy by examining whether key incubator traits are associated with positive tenant performance.

5.2 Theorizing Why Traits Matter: New Business and Incubator Traits

While management scholars have studied and proposed several drivers of performance among new businesses (Aldrich, 1999; Baum, Locke, & Smith, 2001; Hannan & Freeman, 1977), public policy scholarship on the role of entrepreneurship and economic growth has been less conclusive (Fritsch, 2007). By assessing how heterogeneity among incubator practices and traits is associated with tenant performance, this chapter begins to uncover empirical evidence that can help better design entrepreneurship policies. This section outlines why research on the traits of business incubation may be associated with tenant performance. I begin with a summary that contrasts the wealth of research done on firm level traits known to be related to new business performance.

5.2.1   New Business Traits and Performance

Understanding firm survival and growth among new businesses is a common theme in the management literature (Boden & Nucci, 2000; Dencker, Gruber, & Shah, 2009; Gimeno, Folta, Cooper, & Woo, 1997; Lee, Lee, & Pennings, 2001; van Praag, 2003). Scholars have identified myriad aspects of the internal and external environments in which businesses operate that affect their performance. Internally, research shows that young and small businesses face disadvantages that lead them to fail or underperform in comparison to incumbent firms (Geroski, 1995). Studies also reveal that individual traits such as ambition, gender, and ethnicity influence firm performance (Boden & Nucci, 2000; Fairlie & Robb, 2008; Gimeno, Folta *et al.*, 1997). In addition, new businesses with ties to financial, university, and business networks can leverage higher performance from their organizational capabilities (Lee, Lee *et al.*, 2001).

When considering the competitive environment, research shows that industry traits and dynamics matter too. Factors such as environmental dynamism—the extent to which an industry is changing—and munificence—the availability of resources that businesses can access to cope with challenges—affect new venture growth and competitive strategies (Baum, Locke *et al.*, 2001). Industry concentration through agglomeration is another factor known to improve new business survival and growth

(Wennberg & Lindqvist, 2010). While economics, management, and strategy research have paid close attention to individual, firm, and environmental conditions associated with new business performance, these fields and public policy scholars have been less attentive in detailing how different configurations of entrepreneurship programs affect new business performance.

5.2.2   Business Incubation Typologies

Past research on business incubation tends to emphasize typologies of incubators due partly to the tremendous growth seen in the sector, the variety of stakeholders involved in creating incubators, and theoretical reasons (Eshun, 2004; Hackett & Dilts, 2004; Zedtwitz, 2003). However, the focus on incubator typologies has failed to produce findings useful for advancing theory on and practices of business incubators (Eshun, 2004; Hackett & Dilts, 2004). This lack of significant results stems from taxonomies of convenience, which lack theoretical motivations and non-random samples (Eshun, 2004; Hackett & Dilts, 2004).

In a well-designed population-level study of incubators, Eshun (2004) proposed a typology of business incubators that included seven categories: real estate, economic development, technology transfer, industry based, research and development commercialization, social enterprise, and financial investment. Eshun's (2004) work is notable in its use of extensive qualitative methods, which were used to assemble and describe these seven categories of incubators. However, a contradiction in Eshun's results was the finding that the majority of incubators in the study were hybrid incubators. In other words, most incubators fell into multiple categories implying that it was rare to find an incubator that fit neatly into one of Eshun's seven espoused categories. While Eshun's research shows that incubators tend to exhibit heterogeneous goals, practices, and origins, the prevalence of hybrid incubators weakens the argument by placing too much attention on typologies as a key research variable. In this study, I step away from Eshun's emphasis on incubator typologies to focus primarily on traits that can be accurately observed and statistically studied. These include nonprofit status, university affiliations, and network densities.

Nonprofit and For-profit Incubators

Since its beginning, the business incubator industry has split itself into nonprofit and for-profit incubators. In fact, the Batavia Industrial Center, the first incubator in the United States, has operated as a for-profit organization from its beginning. Today, nonprofit incubators dominate the incubation industry due to high levels of state and local public funding and the participation of universities and research institutions interested in benefiting from the commercialization of their R&D. However, approximately 10 percent of incubators operate as for-profit entities and this type of incubator has continued to grow since the 1990s due to investments by venture capital firms and investors (Finer & Holberton, 2002; Johnsrud, Theis, & Bezerra, 2003). In fact, the sample of incubators in this study shows that at least 18% of incubators have been founded as for-profit entities.

Given the bifurcation of incubators into for-profit and nonprofit entities, the question remains which type of incubator generates higher long-term business performance. According to public management scholars, one would expect nonprofit incubators to perform at lower levels than their for-profit counterparts due to goals that are more complex, vague, contradictory, and hard to measure (Lan & Rainey, 1992). This outcome is plausible if one assumes that the single priority of for-profit incubators is to generate a return on investment for their investors, while nonprofit incubators might seek to achieve one or all of the following: stimulate job creation, stimulate redevelopment of a neighborhood, and/or increase the number of women and minority business owners. While for-profit incubators might not withstand losses in the long-term, nonprofit incubators may not need to worry about their financial backing because public funders might tolerate subsidizing operations longer (Hedley, 1998).

Another perspective on how the performance of nonprofit and for-profit incubators might differ comes from scholars who study the economic and sociological reasons for the emergence of nonprofit organizations. For example, DiMaggio and Anheier (1990) argue that consumer demand leads to the creation of nonprofits when a donor is buying services for an unknown third party, the beneficiaries of the service are unable to assess service quality, a fee cannot be traced to a specific unit of service, or the service is too complex for consumers to evaluate its quality. In other words, one can expect for-profits to predominate in markets where the "non-contractible quality" of a good is not valued highly by consumers (Glaeser & Shleifer, 2001). Because the nonprofit sector is built on public trust due to its tax exemption and charitable mission (Salamon, 1999), it is argued that when the quality of a service is important to the consumer but evaluation of quality is difficult to assess that consumers will favor nonprofit service providers (Weisbrod, 1988).

Based on this logic, small businesses that seek high-quality services and trustworthy business transactions would be more inclined to pursue incubation in a nonprofit incubator. Furthermore, one would expect tenants of nonprofit incubators to outperform tenants of for-profit incubators because tenants of nonprofit incubators might scrutinize an incubator's service offerings more carefully before entering an incubation program.

Essentially, the preceding discussion centers on two issues: how does the profit motive affect the operations of incubators and how does information asymmetry affect the sorting of firms into nonprofit as opposed to for-profit incubators. According to descriptive studies of the incubator industry, we know that the profit motive affects operations. Mainly for-profit incubators are tied to venture capitalists who seek to incubate entrepreneurs with a proven record of accomplishment, obtain an equity share in start-ups that are expected to grow quickly, and speed up the time it generally takes a business to reach profitability (Finer & Holberton, 2002; Halkides, 2001; Zedtwitz & Grimaldi, 2006). These interests of for-profit incubators imply they take on a more hands-on approach to the selection (Eshun, 2004), management and development of tenants than nonprofit incubators (Finer & Holberton, 2002) because for-profit incubators want to find new businesses likely to succeed. In contrast, research on nonprofit incubators shows they tend to target tenants facing socioeconomic challenges, businesses with longer time horizons for profitability, and those with limited markets (Finer & Holberton, 2002; Halkides, 2001). In essence, descriptions of for-profit incubators tend to signal that they are less patient toward low or poor economic performance of their tenants in contrast to nonprofit incubators, which have a practice of selecting tenants with high odds of low or poor performance.

> **Hypothesis 1:** Tenants of for-profit incubators will perform at higher levels than tenants of nonprofit incubators.

University Incubators

Audretsch, Keilbach, & Lehmann's (2006) knowledge spillover theory of entrepreneurship offers several lenses through which to view the relationship between economic development and factors that foster entrepreneurship. As stated earlier, knowledge spillovers occur when entrepreneurs appropriate and exploit valuable scientific knowledge. The theory states that a gap exists between available knowledge and economically exploitable knowledge due to under- investment in the selection and identification of opportunities for commercializing knowledge. Because knowledge is difficult to codify and transmit—especially in science and technology fields—its economic value is most easily exploited when information is transmitted through frequent and repeated face-to-face interaction (Audretsch *et al.*, 2006). The difficulty of transmitting knowledge and learning its economic applications makes geographic location a key variable in understanding differences in entrepreneurial growth. Those firms and entrepreneurs that reside closest to sources of knowledge are poised to learn its economic merits first.

In order to help their faculties and students commercialize new research and patented inventions, many research universities sponsor and establish their own incubators. Often these incubators work closely with the university's technology transfer office (Eshun, 2004; Markman, Phan *et al.*, 2005). Because universities create incubators to facilitate knowledge spillovers, it is important to examine the performance behavior of tenants in university led incubators. An assumption based on knowledge spillover theory is that tenants of university led incubators would hold an advantage over tenants of other types of incubators in first learning about important economically valuable knowledge and in getting the technical expertise to commercialize it.

Past research on university incubators has shown that their tenants enjoy several advantages in terms of accessing research, human capital, and technological resources (Rothaermel & Thursby, 2005b). In a study of 79 firms incubated by Georgia Tech University, Rothaermel & Thursby (2005a; 2005b) found that those firms holding a Georgia Tech technology license were less likely to fail. In addition, they found that firms, which cited Georgia Tech's university research, were more likely to receive higher levels of venture capital. While their study spanned the height of the dot-com economic cycle, 1998-2003, and their results might be time-dependent, their findings and methods also show that firms in university incubators that actively exploit local knowledge resources are most successful.

> **Hypothesis 2:** Tenants of university incubators will perform at higher levels than tenants of incubators not affiliated with a university.

Network Externalities

Networks allow entrepreneurs to discover opportunities, test ideas, and garner resources to form businesses (Lee, Lee *et al.*, 2001). The advantages of collaboration within networks include knowledge-sharing, access to complementary skills, and economies of scale (Ahuja, 2000). The benefits of networks to the spurring of entrepreneurship include higher outputs of innovations and faster firm growth (Ahuja, 2000). Networks play a key role in knowledge spillovers as seen in research showing that scientists primarily transfer knowledge to firms with close proximity and offer different types of services to firms located further away (Audretsch, 2003). The geographic importance of networks is also seen in research showing that an entrepreneur's residence influences his or her perception of opportunities (Arenius & Clercq, 2005).

An important outcome of networks is cluster development—the geographic agglomeration of industries—which is known to result in innovation, cooperation, and competition (Ács & Varga, 2005; Enright, 2003). Clusters assist entrepreneurial development because they allow firms to share the risks and rewards of R&D, share tacit knowledge, and lower transaction costs when collaborating (Enright, 2003). These aspects of a strong business climate also create stronger linkages between large and small businesses (Florida, 2003). R&D findings from collaborative research among firms often lead to new start-ups when corporate research sponsors are unwilling to assume the risk of marketing a new technology. Successful clustering enables economic growth through the creation and diffusion of opportunities for new ventures and enhances the survival of small businesses through increased competition (Enright, 2003).

According to the knowledge spillover theory, a network market failure occurs when a region with a population of entrepreneurial firms and individuals fails to develop geographic linkages (Audretsch, Keilbach *et al.*, 2006). Because networks enable collaboration and the diffusion of knowledge and ideas, entrepreneurial firms and individuals can benefit from the processes that networks enable. These processes—collaborative R&D and finding and sorting economically valuable knowledge—help firms discover, transform, and apply scientific research in the production of a new good, improvement in quality of a current good, the use of a more efficient method of production, the opening of a new market for an available good or service, the discovery and ownership of a new supply of raw materials, or the restructuring of an industry (Schumpeter, 1934).

In the context of business incubation, it has been shown that economic development attracts the interest of diverse stakeholders in the community. Cox *et al.* (1991) found that the typical participants in community development policy meetings include representatives from the Chamber of Commerce, city and county governments, banks, development authorities, media, real estate development, and colleges and universities. Indeed, many incubators often host not only for-profit tenants but also nonprofit business associations and economic development agencies, which facilitate the transfer of business skills and information to for-profit tenants.

Qualitative research on business incubators has shown that tenants view networking as an important benefit of incubation (Aernoudt, 2004). Thus far, the literature on networks within incubators focuses on inter-firm collaboration among for-profit tenants and documents how tenants build business and informal mentoring relationships of mutual benefit (Aernoudt, 2004; Bollingtoft & Ulhoi, 2005)

However, the question of how an incubator's economic development and business services network affects tenant performance has not been well studied. It has been posited that an incubator acts as a node point for its tenants, who can easily foster relationships with business services and consultants (McAdam, Galbraith, McAdam, & Humphreys, 2006). Tenants with weak networks—having few ties and weak ties with others—can compensate for their lack of beneficial business relationships by using their incubator's network (Peters, Rice, & Sundararajan, 2004). The use of an incubator's network creates a formal process through which a tenant can quickly be embedded into a beneficial business network that can help increase survival and business performance (McAdam, Galbraith *et al.*, 2006).

> **Hypothesis 3:** Tenants of incubators with a larger economic development network will perform at higher levels than tenants of incubators with a smaller economic development network.

5.2.3 Entrepreneur's Traits

Gender and minority identity effects

Historically, women participation in new venture creation has been disproportionally less than men. For example, women make up 27% of business owners despite their larger participation in the workforce; they are 50% less likely to be involved in starting a new business at any point in time than men; and they make up only 34% of the self-employed (Shane, 2008). Not only are women less involved in entrepreneurship, their businesses tend to underperform. There is much evidence that women owned businesses grow at a lower rate, employ fewer people, are less profitable, and fail more often than those owned by men (Fairlie & Robb, 2008; Shane, 2008). Explanations for why women owned businesses perform at lower levels than those of men point to factors like time devoted to housework and evidence that women devote less time and energy to their businesses than men (Hundley, 2001). In addition, current research on these trends indicates that men and women have different interests and ambitions when starting businesses. For example, Carter *et al.* (2003) find that men rate financial success and innovation higher than women do when asked about reasons for choosing careers. In addition, women often start businesses during motherhood to have flexible work schedules (Shane, 2008).

Just as women are underrepresented in entrepreneurial activities, so are ethnic and racial minorities—specifically, African Americans. While blacks are 78 percent more likely to be in the process of starting a business than whites, their interest in entrepreneurship does not translate into proportionally higher rates of business ownership or self-employment than whites (Shane, 2008). Studies show that lack of financial and human capital are a reason for the low rates of entrepreneurship among African Americans (Fairlie & Robb, 2008). Furthermore, business performance among African American owned enterprises is markedly lower than those owned by whites, just as women owned firms tend to underperform in comparison to men owned firms.

One explanation for the preponderance of underperformance among women and black owned firms is a lack of relevant work experience in a family owned business. In a study of small business performance that controls for gender and racial identities of small new businesses, Fairlie and Robb (2008) found that an entrepreneur with a family history of self-employment and family business ownership tended to outperform entrepreneurs lacking this background. However, the reason for the improved performance did not depend on the entrepreneur's good fortune in having been born into a business-oriented family; it relied on the entrepreneur's relevant involvement in the family's business. In other words, entrepreneurs who gained work experience in a family business were more likely to own strongly performing businesses in comparison to peers who grew up in a family that owned a business but did not work in the business. In their study, Fairlie and Robb (2008) found that among all the entrepreneurs in their sample, women and black entrepreneurs were less likely to have worked in their family's business or have relevant work experience in a small firm. While the authors do not explain why women were less likely to work in a family business than men, they do point out various reasons why black entrepreneurs are less likely to work in a family business than whites. Black families in particular tend to face educational, wealth, and employment disadvantages, which decrease their entrepreneurship startup rates and hamper their business success. Thus, black entrepreneurs are less likely to work in a family business because as a population they are less likely to grow up in families with self-employed family members and family businesses.

Thus, while scholarship shows that women- and minority-owned businesses underperform their male and white counterparts, there is evidence showing that a key reason for this lack of performance stems from a particular type of learning and mentoring that occurs through work in a family business prior to starting one's new venture. Hence, while we might expect women and minority owned incubated firms to underperform in contrast to male and white owned firms, we should also expect women and minority owned firms to benefit differently from incubation. Because incubators exist partly to offer business expertise to their clients and evidence exists that women and minority owned businesses tend to underperform due to a lack of business expertise, I predict that women and minority owned firms will respond at higher levels to the three incubator traits analyzed in this study if these traits are associated with increased business performance.

Hypothesis 4: Women owned incubated businesses will have a stronger performance response to incubation than male owned incubated businesses.

Hypothesis 5: Minority owned incubated businesses will have a stronger performance response to incubation than male owned incubated businesses.

5.3 Data

To test the above hypotheses, I assembled and merged two datasets: a panel of the majority of current and previously known business incubators and a panel of firm-level data from the National Establishment Time-Series Database (NETS) provided by Walls & Associates (Walls, 2009). The unit of analysis is limited to new businesses, which I define as those being under 5 years of age at the time of incubation. This choice is based on the premise that incubators exist to assist vulnerable new businesses overcome the risks of failure in the startup phase.

5.3.1 Business incubator data

The panel of business incubator data consists of 944 business incubators, which have operated in 1,121 establishments. Several online archival methods were used to confirm all known addresses of the incubator, legal status, founding year, dissolution year if applicable, and affiliation with an institution of higher education.

I created the most inclusive and exhaustive population of business incubators possible by collecting membership rosters of the National Business Incubation Association, 23 state associations of business incubators, and economic development resource lists from 50 state governments. Because the majority of business incubators incorporate as nonprofit organizations, I also conducted a search for incubators using the master file database of the National Center for Charitable Statistics (NCCS), a clearinghouse of data on the U.S. nonprofit sector. In addition, two national rosters from the University of Central Florida Business Incubation Program for the years 2007 and 2009 were obtained.

Due to concerns that the population of business incubators overrepresented "successful" and "younger" incubators, those not having closed since incorporation and those most recently formed, an additional search for missing incubators was conducted by Walls & Associates using the NETS. Because approximately 30% of the organizations in the master list contained the term "incubator" in their name, a search was done using the term's root "incubat." The search identified an additional 130 business incubators, many of which had ceased operations prior to data collection.

In order to deduce and verify the incubator's name, physical address, contact information, nonprofit status, university affiliation, and founding year, I relied on the search engine Google (www.google.com) and the Internet Archive (www.archive.org), which stores a digital library of over 150 billion screen shots of web pages dating back to 1996. When my initial online research failed to identify all of the incubator variables of interest, I resorted to using the master file database of NCCS, the D&B Million Dollar Database, and LexisNexis Academic. In all cases, the information reported by the incubator on its website and printed materials was preferred to secondary information provided by a third party database. In special circumstances, where none of the above online research methods led to the confirmation of all variables of interest for each incubator, I resorted to a short e-mail survey to acquire missing data which garnered a 45% response rate.

5.3.2   Firm level data

Because data on failed incubated businesses is more difficult to find than data on successful incubated businesses (Hackett & Dilts, 2004), I chose to extract a sample of all incubated businesses from the NETS using address matching techniques. The NETS is a longitudinal dataset of over 36.5 million business establishments built from annual snapshots of Dun & Bradstreet (D&B) data (Walls, 2009). The NETS includes key geographic, descriptive, and performance data for businesses, such as every known establishment address, industry and legal status codes, founding year, and annual sales and employment figures (Walls, 2009).

D&B defines business establishments as a "business or industrial unit at a single physical location that produces or distributes goods or performs services" (Neumark, Zhang, & Wall, 2005). This characteristic of the NETS database was crucial to conducting an address-based query to extract a population of likely incubated businesses. Using a query which matched the known physical addresses of the business incubator population with the physical addresses of the over 36.5 million business establishments in the NETS, a data extract of approximately 38,000 establishments was pulled. In order to capture the relocation patterns of both businesses and incubators, a second "NETS Moves" dataset detailing the historical record of where firms and incubators had existed was pulled. It is important to note that while the first NETS dataset provided longitudinal performance measures of all firms that were co-located with an incubator, it was not possible to tell precisely whether those behaviors all took place pre-incubation, while in incubation, or post-incubation. The NETS Moves dataset made it possible to determine the year when firms moved into an incubator and when they moved out.

5.3.3   Data merging and manipulation

Assembly of the final dataset required several merger and culling steps, which reduced the initial sample of 38,000 potentially incubated businesses to 19,420. The merger steps were necessary to identify precisely when a business moved into and out of an address and then compare that time period with the time period when an incubator moved into and out of an address. Only in cases where the business and the incubator simultaneously shared the same address did that firm's record become part of the final dataset.

Because in many circumstances incubators inhabit buildings with multiple tenants, I also carefully selected out several types of firms. These include all businesses incorporated as nonprofits and falling under SIC codes for government. Because this study focuses only on the incubation of new and young businesses, I dropped all firms which had existed for longer than five years at the time that their associated incubator was born. In addition, firms with an initial employment of over 100 and those determined to be large corporations were dropped[1]. Finally, all firms which were started

---

[1]Based on the definition of incubation and the entrepreneurship literature, I limit my sample to those firms deemed to be young and small-medium enterprises at the time of incubation. Thus, a young firm implies that the firm is under the age of 5 at the time in which it is born in the incubator or at the time it moves into the incubator. In addition, a small-medium enterprise restriction is used to exclude large public corporations from the analysis. For example, many incubators co-exist in

after an incubator had ceased operations or moved out of a location were dropped as well.

To assess further the accuracy of the address matching process in identifying all former and current tenants of business incubators, a data audit was conducted. A random sample of 65 incubators and their matched tenants (1,200 firms) was pulled from the remaining dataset. I then surveyed the sample of incubators through e-mail asking their managers to report which of the listed firms, were current or former tenants. The survey generated a 49% response rate and revealed that 78% of the listed firms were current or former tenants[2].

5.4 Methodology

5.4.1 Performance Measures

I used three performance measures—sales growth, employment growth, and survival—which were selected for their theoretical and policy implications. Empirically, we know that new businesses are slow to grow and that firm survival is a stronger measure of firm performance when firms are young (Geroski, 1995). Yet, a strong motivation for why policymakers support entrepreneurship programs is the claim made by business incubators that they speed up the growth process, especially in regards to employment, and reduce business failure (Hackett & Dilts, 2004). On the other hand, en-

---

business parks and commercial centers where multinational corporations also exist. I dropped out of the sample all firms which were clearly large corporations operating on their own but happening to share the same building and/or physical address as a business incubator.

[2]It should be noted that through further investigation, I uncovered inaccuracies in the responses from incubators. In some cases, respondents did not recall accurately former clients, especially if the incubator was larger and older and the respondent was new to the incubator's staff. In other cases, responses were misleading. In one case, a respondent reported that several listed businesses were not clients of the incubator but upon calling one of the clients directly, I discovered that the firm was still operating within the incubator. In other cases, I found out through research using the Internet Archive that several businesses that were reported to not have been tenants of an incubator were actually listed as tenants on an incubator's website in prior years. Due to the errors in reporting, I suspect the accuracy of my matching strategy is actually much higher than 78%.

trepreneurs pay most attention to metrics like sales and revenue growth (Davidsson and Wiklund, 2006). Whether incubated new businesses are primed through incubation to grow or survive in the external environment is an important empirical question that can help us develop better entrepreneurship policies and inform practice.

Following much of the firm growth literature which relies heavily on Gibrat's proportional growth model (Coad, 2007a; Sutton, 1997), I defined growth as the log difference in firm size,

$$\text{Growth}_{i,t} = \log(\text{SIZE}_{i,t}) - \log(\text{SIZE}_{i,t-1})$$

Thus, sales growth is the log difference between annual sales at time t and sales at time $t - 1$. Note that annual sales figures were first adjusted to 2008 dollars based on the consumer price index before being log transformed. Similarly, employment figures were first log transformed and then differenced in order to calculate annual employment growth. Firm failure was measured by examining the last year in which a business was active in the NETS. Firm failure is a dummy variable equal to 1 if the last year of activity reported by the NETS is not 2008.

5.4.2 Theorized Explanatory Variables

Nonprofit

As previously noted, nonprofit incubators were identified using several secondary data sources. *Nonprofit* is a dummy variable that is equal to 1 if the incubator is incorporated as a nonprofit and 0 if the incubator is incorporated as a for-profit.

University

University is a dummy variable that is coded 1 if the incubator is sponsored by a university or community college. The variable was derived from reviewing incubator websites and from industry codes associated with each incubator found in the NETS database.

Network

Network is a count of economic development, business, and professional associations that were found to be co-located with the business incubator on an annual basis.

Women Owned

The NETS reports whether a business is women owned. This dummy variable equals 1 for women owned enterprises.

Minority Owned

The variable *minority owned* is a dummy variable where 1 represents a business owned by an entrepreneur who is non-white. Because most of the relevant research on how race and ethnicity affects business ownership and business performance centers on the African-American population, this variable requires cautious interpretation because the NETS data on minority firm ownership does not distinguish between different ethnic and racial subgroups.

5.4.3 Standard Control Variables

I controlled for several firm level effects: size, age, and industry. Because it is generally known that smaller firms tend to grow faster than larger firms, controlling for firm-size effects is important in this model (Coad, 2007b). Therefore, *lagged employment* measures firm size when the dependent variable is *sales growth* and *lagged sales* is a measure of firm size when the dependent variable is *employment growth* or *survival*. Switching measures of firm-size in relation to the dependent variable is necessary to avoid statistical bias due to autocorrelation when a lagged dependent variable is included in the model.

The age of the firm is measured in years. Eight 2-digit SIC dummy codes were used to control for industry effects. These fell into eight broad industries: agriculture, construction, manufacturing, transportation, wholesale trade, retail trade, finance, and services. In addition, year dummies were used to control for overall economic trends. Finally, I included the age of the incubator as a control, expecting to see accumulated improvements in firm performance from older incubators due to accumulated learning and integration into the community (Allen & McCluskey, 1990; Erlewine & Gerl, 2004). Table B.17 lists descriptive statistics on all dependent and explanatory variables.

5.4.4   Estimation Procedures

Survival Analysis

Survival analysis is commonly used to study the occurrence of failure over time among subjects while controlling various treatments and demographic characteristics (Wooldridge, 2002). In this study, I use a parametric model with a Weibull distribution. Several distributions were tested for fit. I chose the Weibull model because it had the largest log likelihood and the lowest Akaike Information Criterion value (Cleves, 2008). I also decided to use a parametric model as opposed to a proportional hazard model because assuming a distribution allows for full use of all observations and makes it possible to account for time-varying covariates (Cleves, 2008).

The functional form of the proportional hazards regression model using a Weibull distribution is given as (Cleves, 2008):

$$h(t|x_j) = \exp(\beta_0 + \beta_x x_j)t^p$$

In this model, p represents a scale parameter that is estimated by exponentiation of the estimated intercept coefficient (β_0) which is also a measure of the baseline hazard, $h_0(t)$. The parameter is an indicator of hazards that exhibit increasing or decreasing rates over time (Cleves, 2008). Assuming a functional form of $h_0(t)$ makes sense in this study since it is generally known that failure rates of start-up firms decrease over time (Shane, 2008). β_x represents the vector of coefficients that are to be estimated (Cleves, 2008). In the above model, $\exp(\beta_x x_j)$ represents the following terms which are similar as in the sales and employment growth model above.

$$
\begin{aligned}
h(t|x_j) = \quad & \beta_1 pre\text{-}incubation_{i,t} + \beta_2 incubation_{i,t} + \beta_3 nonprofit_{i,j} + \\
& \beta_4 network_{i,j,t} + \beta_5 university_{i,j} + (\beta_6 npo_{i,j} \times inc_{i,t}) + \\
& (\beta_7 network_{i,j,t} \times inc_{i,t}) + (\beta_8 uni_{i,j} \times inc_{i,t}) + \beta_9 women_i + \beta_{10} minority_i + \\
& (\beta_{11} wom_{i,j} \times inc_{i,t}) + (\beta_{12} min_{i,j} \times inc_{i,t}) + \beta_{13} incubator\ age_{i,j,t} + \\
& \beta_{14} firm\ age_{i,t} + \beta_{15} lag\ size_{i,t} + \beta_{16-24} industry_{i,t}
\end{aligned}
$$

Sales and Employment Growth

Panel data analysis is often used for policy evaluation because it has been shown to reduce statistical bias due to omitted variables and unobserved, time-constant factors that affect the dependent variable and are correlated with explanatory variables (Wooldridge, 2006). However, in the case of dynamic growth models where a future value of growth is partially dependent on a current value of growth, it becomes important to adapt panel methods to address issues of endogeneity, serial autocorrelation, and heteroscedasticity. Additionally, the estimated model must address the problem of endogeneity due to reverse causation between unobserved tenant attributes and incubator traits.

Because several explanatory variables in this study are time-invariant, I use the Hausman-Taylor generalized IV estimator, a type of random effects estimator (Cameron & Trivedi, 2009; Wooldridge, 2002). This estimator requires making a strong assumption of orthogonality between the unobserved fixed effect α_i and specific time varying variables (Wooldridge, 2002). When the number of exogenous time varying regressors exceeds the number of endogenous time invariant variables, the values of the exogenous regressors can be used as instruments except in the current period and permit estimation of the endogenous time invariant regressors (Cameron & Trivedi, 2009). Because the Hausman-Taylor generalized IV estimator uses a within panel mean of x_{it}, a within transform estimate of x_{it}, and the vector of exogenous time invariant variables as instruments for the endogenous variables, identification and estimation of models is facilitated. When the model is under identified, results will be equivalent to a fixed effect estimator. The key to estimating the effects of time-invariant variables lies in the use of a random-effects transformation that does not difference away the fixed effect constant, α_i, thus allowing for instrumental variable estimation to address the correlation between the fixed effect and time-varying and time-invariant variables in the generalized model. The estimated model is the follow-ing:

$$
\begin{aligned}
y_{i,t} = \quad & \gamma_1 y_{i,t-1} + \beta_2 incubation_{i,t} + \beta_3 pre\text{-}incubation_{i,j} + \beta_4 nonprofit_{i,j} + \\
& \beta_5 network_{i,j,t} + \beta_6 university_{i,j} + (\beta_7 npo_{i,j} \times inc_{i,t}) + \\
& (\beta_8 uni_{i,j} \times inc_{i,t}) + \beta_9 network_{i,j,t} \times inc_{i,t}) + \beta_{10} women_i + \beta_{11} minority_i + \\
& (\beta_{12} women_i \times inc_{i,t}) + (\beta_{13} minority_i \times inc_{i,t}) + \beta_{14} incubator\ age_{i,j,t} + \\
& \beta_{15} firm\ age_{i,t} + \beta_{16} lag\ size_{i,t} + \beta_{17-24} industry_{i,t} + \gamma_{2t} + \alpha_i + \epsilon_{i,t}
\end{aligned}
$$

In this model, $y_{i,t}$ represents either sales or employment growth, which is lagged as an explanatory variable. Firms are represented by i, incubators by j, and year by t. Incubator characteristics are represented by variables—*npo, network, uni,* and *age*—which are interacted with periods when the firm is incubation. The variable *incubation* is a dummy that represents when the firm resides within the incubator and *pre-incubation* is a dummy variable that represents the period when a firm is born but not yet incubated. The rest of the variables are standard control variables for industry and time.

5.5   Results

5.5.1   Effect of incubator traits on the hazard of firm failure

Table B.18 presents five separate estimates with exponentiated coefficients of the effect of incubator traits on tenants' likelihood to fail. Model 1 represents the base model without interactions. Models 2 and 3 focus on the effects of nonprofit status, university led incubators, and network effects on firm survival. Model 4 emphasizes the effects of incubation on minority and women led firms and model 5 includes all hypothesized variables and their corresponding interactions. Also, a global F-test of all estimated parameters was conducted for each model and results supported rejection of the null hypothesis, indicating that at least one of the estimated parameters was linearly associated with survival.

Focusing on model 4 with the lowest AIC value, results reveal that as tenants of incubators age, their likelihood of failure decreases by 82%, a trend that is common in survival analysis of firms. In addition, in periods of incubation, tenants see their hazard rate decrease by 17% signaling that incubation appears to reduce failure rates. Additionally, the coefficient *incubator age* confirms the results from Allen and Mc-Cluskey (1990), who found that the performance of tenants increased with the age of the incubator. The effect is small, a 1% decrease in the likelihood of failure, but highly significant.

Turning attention to analysis of hypothesized effects, I found no evidence to support the view that tenants of for-profit incubators are more likely to survive than tenants of nonprofit incubators. The effect fluctuates between reducing and increasing the likelihood of failure depending on whether interactions with incubation are included, indicating possible problems with unobserved heterogeneity associated with selection into a nonprofit business incubator.

Model 4 does offer evidence that tenants of university led incubators perform better than tenants of non-university incubators. Overall, models 4 and 2 show that tenants of university led incubators face a hazard rate that is 17% lower than tenants of other incubators. This finding supports the conclusion of the knowledge spillover theory that predicts that being closer to a source of knowledge increases a firm's ability to exploit the economic value of new knowledge. However, one should be cautious to attribute the strength and significance of this effect to the incubator and not the university setting since models 3 and 5 do not provide significant results. *University* in models 3 and 5 account for the latent effect of having been incubated in a university sponsored incubator, while *uni* $\times$ *inc* accounts for the actual period of time when the firm resided in a university incubator.

Looking at whether an incubator's network of business and economic development associations helps their tenants survive, I found evidence against hypothesis 3. All the models reveal that an increase in one additional member to an incubator's business association network increases the likelihood of failure. The negative effect of networks vary according to whether the term is interacted with *incubation*. However, none of the interactions are significant.

While networks don't affect tenant survival during incubation directly, the findings reveal that incubators that host greater numbers of economic development peers face declining economies of scale in performance. These findings may reflect the role that networks of incubators play in attracting certain types of tenants to incubation. Also, the finding implies that agglomeration of business associations does not lead to a greater transfer of business knowledge and an increase in survival of tenants.

While the results do not imply that a larger network directly causes higher rates of failure among tenants of incubators, it does imply that their anticipated benefits are not achieved. Further research should be done to understand whether this is due to the structure of these networks. For example, it maybe that these networks also see incubators as places to conduct business cheaply and not as places to leverage their services. It also may be that strong likelihood of failure due to network size is also related to selection processes where tenants of incubators are unprepared to leverage these additional services.

Based on model 4, it is striking to find that incubated minority owned firms face tremendously poor odds of survival. While in the baseline model, they face a 20% higher rate of failure than white owned firms, in model 4 the likelihood of failure increases to over 300%. However, taking into account time in which minority owned firms are in incubation, their risk of failure falls significantly to a rate that is only 11% higher than white owned firms. While minority owned firms represent a miniscule percentage of overall tenants of business incubators, these figures point out that perhaps other business support programs are needed to help minority owned firms in incubators. It is not surprising that minority owned firms, or any firm for that matter, face a lower risk of failure while being incubated, but it is troubling to note that in times when minority owned firms are not in incubation their hazard rates are dramatically higher. This overall higher likelihood of failure of minority owned firms verifies similar results where the race of the owner is controlled for in evaluating firm performance (Fairlie & Robb, 2008).

The effects of incubation on the survival of women owned firms reveals some complexities. First, the baseline model indicates that women owned firms in the sample face better odds of survival. Their likelihood of failure is 38% less than that of men owned firms. Similar conclusions can be drawn from models 2 and 3. However, once the time of incubation of women owned firms is taken into account, as in models 4 and 5, the baseline effect is no longer significant. If the baseline effect had remained significant, women owned firms while in incubation would face a 36% lower likelihood of failure in comparison to men owned firms. A possible explanation for this shifting nature of significance is that the majority of observations in the data are those of firms in the state of incubation, making it harder to estimate the baseline effects. Overall, the hazard rates on women actually reveal favorable findings regarding the performance of women owned firms that are tenants of incubators. This implies that women owned businesses are perhaps a better fit for incubation programs and that gender differences in how women approach new business creation lead them to succeed more than men in an incubator environment.

5.5.2   Effect of incubator traits on employment growth

Table B.19 presents the estimates of the effect of incubator traits on *employment growth*. A global F-test of all estimated parameters for each model indicated that at least one of the estimated parameters was linearly associated with employment growth. Overall, the strongest effects on an incubated business's employment growth are its size, measured in annual sales, and its employment growth rate in the previous year. The coefficients in the base model are large and their magnitude and significance persist across all five models. The coefficients are negative, implying that as incubated businesses increase in size and their growth accelerates, their employment growth decreases. These results are similar to findings in the firm growth literature (Coad, 2007b; Sutton, 1997) and indicate that incubated businesses generally demonstrate the same tendencies of firms in other studies on growth.

Another interesting finding is that this population of incubated businesses appears to have a tendency to be in decline prior to incubation and while in incubation. Both coefficients are negative across the models but only the *pre-incubation* indicator is significant.

Focusing on model 3 with the largest chi-squared value, it becomes apparent that tenants of for-profit incubators outperform tenants of nonprofit incubators in employment growth. Having been incubated by a nonprofit incubator has a large negative effect on employment growth for incubated businesses. The tenants of nonprofit incubators generally have employment growth rates that are 200% less than those of tenants of for-profit incubators. These expected results indicate that nonprofit incubators serve firms that likely have different growth aspirations or ability than those firms incubated by for-profit incubators. It is also important to note that across all the models, interactions of hypothesized variables with *incubation* are not significant.

Results show that tenants of university incubators experience much higher levels of employment growth than firms incubated in non-university led incubators. Overall, tenants of university incubators experience employment growth that is 370% higher than that of firms incubated in non-university led incubators. The results signal that tenants of university incubators are perhaps benefiting from the additional knowledge resources and facilities available to them in institutions of higher education. Like in the survival model, the correlation between positive performance and incubation in a university incubator may imply a location effect as opposed to an incubation effect since the interaction term is not significant. Whether this positive effect on employment growth is due to incubation, access to talent in the form of trained students and scholars, or produced knowledge in the form of patent licensing or published research is a question that should be further investigated.

Hypothesis 3 posits that tenants of incubators with a larger business association network would perform at higher levels than tenants of incubators with a smaller business association network. The results provide support, albeit limited, for this hypothesis. Across all models, the coefficient for network is positive, small in size, and significant in two of the models. Thus, for every new member added to an incubator's network, the contribution to employment growth is less than 1%. Thus, hypothesis 3 is weakly supported.

In general, women owned incubated businesses appear to have higher levels of employment growth than their men owned counterparts. The coefficient *women* is positive and small across four of the models but only significant in model 3. The coefficient in model 3 implies that women owned incubated firms tend to have an employment growth level that is 8% higher than men owned firms. Looking at the interaction effects between women owned firms and being in incubation, the results are small and not significant. Hence, there is weak evidence that incubation plays an important role in the performance of women owned incubated businesses.

The estimates of how minority owned firms perform do not support hypothesis 5 and reveal that this group of incubated businesses actually perform better in comparison to white owned firms. The coefficients for the term *minority* are generally positive, somewhat large especially in models 2 and 3, but not always significant. Furthermore, there is no evidence that, when in an incubator, minority owned firms fare much better since the interaction with incubation is not significant. What is notable about the findings is that the group of minority owned firms in this study do not reflect trends of minority owned firms that is seen in other literature (Fairlie & Robb, 2008). Usually, one would expect firms owned by blacks to perform at lower levels than those owned by whites. Because performance has been shown to vary according to more nuanced measures of racial and ethnic identity, these results might be more telling if I could have undertaken an analysis solely looking at racial and ethnic differences between entrepreneurs.

5.5.3   Effect of incubator traits on sales growth

Table B.20 presents the estimates of the effect of incubator traits on *sales growth*. A global F-test of all estimated parameters for each model indicated that at least one of the estimated parameters was linearly associated with *sales growth*. In the base model, results show that the strongest effect on an incubated business's sales growth is its growth rate in the previous year. The coefficient is large and negative. Also, results indicate that firms originating outside an incubator faced declining sales growth as indicated by the negative and significant coefficient on the variable *pre-incubation*.

Across models 2 to 5, strong evidence exists to support hypothesis 1. Tenants of nonprofit incubators experience sales growth that is approximately 130% lower than that of tenants of for-profit incubators. This finding points to fact that tenants of nonprofit incubators are different in their growth aspirations and ability in comparison to tenants of for-profit incubators. It is also important to note that the interaction of nonprofit status with incubation is negative but not significant.

Further support of hypothesis 2 is seen in the large and highly significant co-efficients for *university* variables in models 2 to 5. Sales growth among tenants of university incubators is at least 200% higher than that of tenants of non-university led incubators. This finding coincides with the results in the employment growth and hazard models. There is overwhelming evidence among the three models that an incubated business in close proximity to a university campus tends to experience higher levels of performance.

Hypothesis 3 posits that tenants of incubators with a larger business association network would perform at higher levels than tenants of incubators with a smaller business association network. Models 2 to 5 provide evidence in support of the hypothesis; however, the effect is miniscule (less than 1% increase in growth).

Hypothesis 3 is a further test of the knowledge spillover theory of entrepreneurship, which asserts that locations with a high density of networks that support the transmission of tacit knowledge and information will have higher levels of entrepreneurship. In this study, this assertion is being studied in terms of networks that support business development.

Overall the evidence for hypothesis 3 is weak and implies that larger business and economic development networks contribute little to the increase in performance of incubated businesses. Across all three measures of performance, networks appear to have a competing effect that varies according to each measure. In the hazard model, larger networks face declining economies of scale that increase the likelihood of failure. When *networks* is regressed on *sales growth* and *employment growth*, the effect then becomes slightly positive.

The results from the three measures of performance do not provide strong evidence in favor of hypothesis 3 that networks further enhance the transfer of knowledge. The results can imply that perhaps the effect of networks on firm performance vary according the type of knowledge transfer that is being measured. Hence, networks based on industry or research may generate different findings than measures of business association networks.

Another explanation of these results comes from social network theory. It is known that entrepreneurs generally seek and need knowledge to first identify promising business ideas and then to acquire the resources and expertise necessary to successfully launch the business (Aldrich, 1999). When entrepreneurs lack close relationships to sources of knowledge, they can overcome this barrier by seeking brokers—people and organizations—who can facilitate links between two individuals (Aldrich, 1999). In this study, business incubators and their co-located peers can be considered two types of brokers and perhaps even be redundant in their knowledge and external networks. Social network theory views homogenous networks, those with many redundant ties, as decreasing in value as the network grows. This is because of the assumption that in these networks there is less new information being transmitted, all new information quickly gets transmitted, and evaluation of new information is generally homogenous (Aldrich, 1999). Because the network variable essentially captures how many other business development peers are co-located with the incubator, it tests the redundant effects of business development services.

The sales growth model provides limited evidence towards hypothesis 4. The estimated coefficients for women owned firms in models 2 and 3 show that women owned firms tend to experience a 8% growth in sales overall in comparison to men owned firms. However, when accounting for the interaction with *incubation*, the significance of the *women* owned variables drops. This implies that the group of women owned firms in this study might perform more strongly than their men owned counterparts, but there is no evidence that incubation contributes directly to the outcome.

Likewise, the estimates for minority owned variables show similar results. However, none of the coefficients are significant.

5.6 Conclusion

This study is one of the first to attempt to observe the performance of a large population of incubators and their affiliated tenants. The focus on how incubator traits are related to tenant performance is interesting for theoretical and practical reasons. Incubators play a key role in the entrepreneurial activities of local communities and their evolution over time has resulted in many permutations to the incubation model. For example, the growth of for-profit and university led incubators are important trends in the field. At the same time, theories of entrepreneurship point toward the importance of knowledge spillovers by leveraging research and network resources. Thus, knowing whether certain attributes of incubators are associated with better performance among tenants of incubators can help scholars better understand theories of entrepreneurial economic growth and generate evidence that can inform the practice of incubation.

In this study, I have shown that incubated businesses in university incubators outperform their peers. To understand further the benefits of knowledge spillovers provided by university incubators future studies should attempt to control for other firm- and incubator- level factors. In terms of firms, scholars should look at whether high technology firms benefit more from university incubation than service industry firms. Also, controlling for technology license agreements, patents, and new research being acquired by the firm from the university can distinguish to what extent technical and proprietary knowledge may matter. This can be contrasted to tacit and professional knowledge that university tenants may acquire by employing students and faculty (Rothaermel & Thursby, 2005a, 2005b).

At the incubator level, scholars might look at whether university incubators are specialized in a specific field of research, new technology, or professional service. For example, some university incubators are sponsored by offices to technology transfer, others by specific schools or colleges, and others by stand-alone research centers. In addition, researchers can also look at whether the variance in goals of university incubators affects tenant performance. For example, some university incubators devote themselves to teaching entrepreneurship to students while others are created to foster entrepreneurship among the faculty. The finding that university led incubators attract higher-performing tenants should receive more attention from scholars interested in the role of human capital and entrepreneurial performance, innovation and economic growth, and emerging technologies.

Some limitations in the study pertain to the measurement of some key variables. Specifically, the variable *minority* does not distinguish between different subgroups and *university* does not distinguish between teaching and research institutions. Additionally, the study relies on the assumption that incubated businesses can be correctly identified through address matching. While this assumption was tested through a data audit that showed that over 78% of matched firms were indeed incubated, errors in the identification of incubated businesses contribute to estimation bias. Furthermore, future attempts to understand the relationship between incubation models and the performance of their tenants should address the challenges of selection bias with more robust methods. In this study, an instrumental variables approach that uses generalized least squares and within transformations to estimate the endogenous parameters was used. This allowed me to circumvent identification of more relevant instruments, a choice made due to the large-scale nature of the panel data.

Overall, the study makes an important contribution to the evaluation of entrepreneurship programs and policies. If communities are to improve their stewardship of limited economic development funds, more research on timely topics such as incubation are needed to focus programs and resources towards increasing the performance of small and young firms.

Chapter 6

Conclusion

If there is a silver lining to the economic crisis our country faces, it is the tremendous attention now paid to job creation and economic growth from policy makers and academics as well as everyday citizens. For far too long the sources of job creation in our economy have been taken for granted.

— ROBERT STROM, Director, Research & Policy, Kauffman Foundation
March 17, 2010 hearing of the House Committee on Small Business

After decades of growth in the business incubation industry, stemming from private and federal, state, and local government investments in business incubation programs, this dissertation probed two important questions often asked about incubation:

1. Do incubated businesses outperform their unincubated peers?

2. Does the economic performance of incubated businesses vary according to design characteristics of incubators and attributes of the entrepreneur?

This conclusion summarizes the findings of the dissertation and identifies areas for future research on business incubation. I encourage others to study the outcomes and practices of business incubation using objective data and robust methods in order to decipher further the startling findings of this dissertation. These include learning that business incubation leads new ventures to failure sooner than otherwise predicted;

that university incubators generate higher performing tenants than non-university sponsored incubators; and that women owned incubated firms outperform men owned incubated firms. As the need for economic growth increases, the findings of this study layout new approaches for tailoring entrepreneurship policy. In addition, the findings shed light on several organization, entrepreneurship, and economic theories and their implications may lead to further theory development.

Do incubated firms outperform their unincubated peers?

To answer the first question, I gathered the most comprehensive sample of business incubators and incubated ventures ever attempted and compared the performance of incubated businesses to a matched control group of unincubated businesses. I evaluated differences in performance by studying survival, employment growth, and sales growth among incubated and unincubated businesses, using panel data estimation techniques that controlled for location, time, industry, and firm fixed effects.

In the first study, I found that the effects of incubation are deleterious to the long-term survival of new ventures. Incubated businesses outperform their peers in terms of employment and sales growth but fail sooner. When a firm enters an incubator, its lifespan decreases by 2% in comparison to its unincubated analog. Furthermore, when a firm graduates or exits an incubator, its lifespan decreases by 10% compared to a firm that stays in incubation. While these findings are unexpected, they do not imply that incubation is bad policy. Signaling and guidance that incubated businesses receive under close monitoring in an incubator may speed up selection processes (Aldrich, 1999) that weed out failing businesses much sooner than the market would.

In terms of growth, the first study revealed that incubated businesses see their employment growth rate increase by 3.5 percentage points in comparison to unincubated businesses. Furthermore, when these firms graduate from the incubator, their employment growth rate increases by 6.65 percentage points. A similar pattern of increased growth rates was observed in terms of sales.

When I examined the long-term effects of incubation using predicted survival, employment growth, and sales growth rates, the findings were discouraging. Specifically, the predictions show that incubation dampens a firm's employment and sales losses. While lossess in employment and sales are lower for incubated businesses in comparison to unincubated firms, the overall effect of incubation does not result in growth. Furthermore, the unincubated firm is expected to stay in business longer. Therefore, the study reveals that incubation does not reverse the ongoing trend of economic and employment decline that is ubiquitous among new ventures (Coad, 2007b; Geroski, 1995; Sutton, 1997). Furthermore, incubated firms that graduate from an incubator have lower levels of employment than the control group, signaling that incubated firms that graduate from an incubator are worse off than had they never been incubated.

This first study of the dissertation contributes to theory development and testing by investigating whether incubation helps new ventures overcome the liability of newness (Shepherd, Douglas, & Shanley, 2000) and increase selection and performance in the external environment (Aldrich, 1999). The positive effect of *incubation* on *sales growth* and *employment growth* provide strong evidence that incubation helps firms reduce the liability of newness. Additionally, the positive effect of *post-incubation* on *sales growth* and *employment growth* shows that incubation helps new ventures adapt to environmental selection forces since an incubated firm grows at a faster pace after exiting the incubator. However, I cannot conclude that incubation helps new ventures surmount the liability of newness and forces of external competitive selection, since incubation leads firms to fail sooner than if they had not been unincubated. Firms in incubation die at a faster pace than their unincubated counterparts and also die off at much faster pace after exiting the incubator. While the findings reveal that incubation programs help new ventures increase employment and sales, they also show that incubation does not generate the net gains in employment, sales, and new ventures that the incubation industry and policymakers desire. Incubated businesses, like their unincubated counterparts, are perpetually in decline and their survival and growth is likely tied to the subsidies of space and training that they receive. Furthermore, since only 4% of incubated businesses graduate from an incubator, the study shows that incubators are failing to wean their tenants off the economic benefits that incubation provides. More research is needed to develop practices that incubators could adopt to strengthen and bolster the performance and survival of their tenants once they exit the incubator.

Does the economic performance of incubated businesses vary according to design characteristics of incubators and attributes of the entrepreneur?

The second question of this dissertation probes whether idiosyncratic characteristics of incubators and entrepreneurs influence the performance of incubated businesses. This question emphasizes the effectiveness of incubation practices rather than the effectiveness of a public policy. To answer this second question, I relied on the same sample of incubators and incubated businesses as in the first study. Estimation techniques in this study relied on panel data methods that enabled estimation of time invariant characteristics of incubators and entrepreneurs, which were potentially correlated with the unobserved characteristics of incubated businesses.

In the second study, I found that tenants of university-sponsored incubators are 17% less likely to fail and have employment growth and sales growth rates that are 370% and 200% higher, respectively, than tenants of other types of incubators. These findings supported the hypothesis that incubators sponsored by a university facilitate knowledge spillovers that give their tenants an advantage in comparison to firms incubated in non-university sponsored incubators. The findings signal that incubators that adopt a strategy of working closely with universities will likely raise the performance of their tenants. Given that university-sponsored incubators represent 27% of the incubator population, proactive measures to increase collaboration between incubators and universities may lead to better performance for the business incubation industry and their tenants in the long-run.

In this study, I also took into account an incubator's network size—measured as the number of business, economic development, and industry associations and nonprofits that were co-located with the incubator. The findings revealed that for each additional member of an incubator's network, a tenant's likelihood of failure increased by 2.5% and the tenant's employment growth and sales growth rates decreased by less than 1%. This startling finding indicates that additional industry and management expertise within incubators does not improve the performance of incubated new ventures. This finding is perhaps explained by social network theory, which predicts that redundant networks often do not add additional value since they lack diversity of thought and information (Aldrich, 1999). Additional research on other attributes of incubator's networks is necessary to explain why this study found networks of industry, business, and economic development experts a detriment to a tenant's performance.

In the second study, I also looked at whether tenants of nonprofit incubators outperform tenants of for-profit incubators. I found out that tenants of for-profit incubators outperform tenants of nonprofit incubators in terms of employment growth and sales growth. Tenants of nonprofit incubators have employment growth and sales growth rates that are 200% and 130% lower respectively. Qualitative studies on business incubators have noticed that nonprofit and for-profit incubators differ in their selection practices and operating goals. A possible explanation for the findings is that nonprofit incubators select tenants where the entrepreneur is less experienced and the new venture is of higher risk. Further study is required to determine what challenges nonprofit incubators and their tenants face. Additionally, this finding implies that the incubation industry may be able to raise the performance of its programs by adopting practices of for-profit incubators or expanding the population of for-profit incubators, since for-profit incubators make up less than 20% of the incubator population.

The data used in this study made it possible to look into two specific traits of entrepreneur's: gender and minority identity. Empirical research has generally found that women entrepreneurs and minority entrepreneurs, especially African-Americans, launch businesses with lower rates of success (Fairlie & Robb, 2008). Explanations emphasize differing goals, lack of industry experience, and lower assets at the outset. I found that minority-owned incubated businesses are 11% more likely to fail than white-owned incubated businesses. However, minority-owned incubated businesses outperform white-owned incubated firms in employment growth: their employment growth rates are 29% higher. Despite the desire of business incubators and policy-makers to bolster economic development in impoverished communities that are often predominantly minority communities as well, the data show that minority-owned incubated businesses make up a miniscule percentage of all incubated firms, 0.5% or 923 of the 19,000 incubated firms. A focus on recruiting and supporting talented minority entrepreneurs is needed to address these discrepancies.

In terms of how women entrepreneurs fare in incubation, the second study found that women owned firms benefit tremendously from incubation services. They are 38% less likely to fail in comparison to men owned firms and experience sales and employment growth rates that are 8% higher than those of men owned firms. Further research is needed to identify the reasons why women owned firms thrive in incubation in comparison to their male counterparts. Additionally, this finding points to another strategy that business incubators may adopt to improve on their past performance. Given that women entrepreneurs respond positively to incubation services, incubators may attempt to increase the percentage of women owned firms that they incubate. Based on the sample of firms in this study, women owned firms comprise 8% of the firms incubated nationally. There is certainly more work that incubators could do to attract and support women owned enterprises.

Future Research Opportunities

Overall, this dissertation contributes to the business incubation industry and to scholarship on entrepreneurship policy by assessing the effectiveness of business incubators. As local, state, and federal governments look for policy solutions to stimulate economic growth and prevent the decline of once-prosperous communities, they are turning to entrepreneurship. Yet, for too long, government leaders and communities have earnestly assumed that business incubation works. This dissertation raises doubts about the assumed effectiveness of business incubation. Despite weaknesses embodied in this study, it is unlikely that it failed to uncover other large positive effects of incubation. The breadth of the data, the multiple relevant measures of firm performance, and the rigor of analytical techniques were extensively vetted to generate robust and generalizable findings.

Besides business incubation, there is a host of other policies and programs across the United States that governments assume also stimulate entrepreneurial activities. These include state-sponsored venture capital funds, small business loan programs, small business development centers, empowerment zones, and business planning programs, among others. The level of adequate research on these other entrepreneurship policy programs is also underdeveloped for guiding decision-making at the policy level and improving management of these programs.

The scholarly and public policy community needs to invest more resources to learning what leads to successful entrepreneurship policy design and the management of entrepreneurship programs. At the macro level, the benefits of entrepreneurship to economic growth are well detailed (Ács & Armington, 2006; Audretsch, Keilbach, & Lehmann, 2006). What's missing are well-designed studies of a qualitative and quantitative nature that shed light on what is necessary to raise the performance of entrepreneurship programs and policies at the local level.

This dissertation meets some of these gaps in knowledge, but the work is not complete. In the future, scholars should look at questions such as:

- Does industry clustering and specialization within incubators lead to stronger tenant performance?

- Does the industry of an incubated business determine whether it exits the incubator successfully?

- Why are women owned firms more successful than men owned firms?

- How do local economic conditions such as poverty, education levels, and industry concentration affect the effectiveness of an incubator program?

- What do failed incubated entrepreneurs learn from having been incubated? Specifically, what benefits—financial, professional, or personal—did they receive from having been incubated?

- Given the choice of investing in alternative entrepreneurship policies, which ones are most likely to produce desired results based on local economic conditions?

Just as research on entrepreneurship itself used to be scare a decade ago, research on entrepreneurship policy remains nascent. Collaboration between public administration, economics, engineering, and management scholars is needed to tackle many of these questions because each brings an important set of methods, theories, and applied implications. Regardless of the findings, such as in this study where not all the findings are encouraging, scholars should seek to answer questions that test interesting theoretical assumptions and inform practice.

Despite finding that business incubators do not achieve their purported successes, the answers to the two questions of this dissertation give scholars and practitioners explanations and propositions that could be tested and debated to help the business incubation industry improve its performance. I hope these findings and their implications are taken into consideration by many in the policymaking community, the business incubation industry, and future scholars of this topic.

www.ingramcontent.com/pod-product-compliance
Lightning Source LLC
LaVergne TN
LVHW041325200726
843509LV00009B/609